Storytelling

How to Create Persuasive Business Presentations

Dave McKinsey

Copyright © 2014 by SpeakingSherpa LLC. All rights reserved. Printed in the United States of America. Except as permitted under the United States Copyright Act of 1976, no part of this publication may be reproduced or distributed in any form or by any means, or stored in a database or retrieval system, without the prior written permission of the author.

In adherence with the "fair use" rule of United States copyright law, this book makes use of materials owned by the United States Postal Service and created by McKinsey & Company, Accenture, and The Boston Consulting Group for the purpose of criticism and commentary and for the purpose of providing a public good by elevating the presentation skills of business professionals. Though I have no direct affiliation with any of these organizations, it is my hope that this book significantly increases the number of people exposed to these organizations and their best practices. All company and product names mentioned herein are the trademarks or registered trademarks of their respective owners.

Printed in the United States by CreateSpace

ISBN: 1500594466

ISBN-13: 978-1500594466

CreateSpace Independent Publishing Platform

North Charleston, South Carolina

Contents

Contents iii

Introduction v

    Chapter 1:   The Perfect Storm 1

Section 1: Persuasive Content 4

    Chapter 2:   The Situation-Complication-Resolution Framework 5

    Chapter 3:   McKinsey's USPS Situation 22

    Chapter 4:   McKinsey's USPS Complication 46

    Chapter 5:   McKinsey's USPS Resolution 61

    Chapter 6:   The Approach-Findings-Implications Framework 84

    Chapter 7:   BCG's USPS Approach 86

    Chapter 8:   BCG's USPS Findings 93

    Chapter 9:   BCG's USPS Implications 104

    Chapter 10:   The Situation-Opportunity-Resolution Framework 114

    Chapter 11:   Accenture's USPS Situation 117

Chapter 12:	Accenture's USPS Opportunity	136
Chapter 13:	Accenture's USPS Resolution	162
Chapter 14:	The Pilot-Results-Scale Framework	169

Section 2: Data-Driven Design 173

Chapter 15:	To Slide or Not to Slide	174
Chapter 16:	Text	186
Chapter 17:	Graphs	199
Chapter 18:	Tables	224
Chapter 19:	Images and Diagrams	229

Section 3: Confident Delivery 240

| Chapter 20: | Verbal Delivery | 241 |
| Chapter 21: | Non-Verbal Delivery | 244 |

Final Words 248

Strategic Storytelling Quick Reference Guide 249

Acknowledgements 256

About the Author 257

Introduction

When I look at the public speaking books piled high on my bookshelf, I notice two patterns and one major gap.

The first pattern is that most public speaking books focus on keynote content and delivery. While there is no strict definition, keynote speeches are highly rehearsed, one-way, motivational, and delivered while standing on a podium in front of an unfamiliar audience. TED Talks and Toastmasters speeches, presentation types on which I have written books, fall into this category.

The second pattern is that presentation design books also fall into the keynote speech category. Two of my favorite authors, Garr Reynolds and Nancy Duarte, set the gold standard for how to craft beautiful presentations. If you have not already, devour everything they have written.

The motivation for focusing on keynotes is compelling: Keynotes are complex, nerve-wracking presentations. Many believe you can excel in any speaking situation if you can deliver an exceptional keynote. However, this logic is flawed.

The truth is that most presentations are delivered at work in seemingly low stakes situations – in the hallway, in one-on-one discussions, and in small group meetings. They are (most of the time) lightly rehearsed, two-way, fact-laden, and delivered while sitting down to a very familiar audience. In short, they are precisely the opposite of keynote speeches.

But, aren't there plenty of books on public speaking at work? Yes and no. The issue is that business-centric public speaking books, as valuable as they have been to me, are often rather academic. Excellent examples covering content and delivery include Stephen Lucas's "The Art of Public Speaking" and Barbara Minto's "The Minto Pyramid Principle." Excellent examples covering design include Gene Zelazny's classic "Say It with Charts" and Stephen Few's essential "Show Me the Numbers."

So, what is the gap I observe while staring at my bookshelf? I want to read a public speaking book that is about the real speaking situations in which I find myself at work every day. I want to read a public speaking book that is entertaining. I want to read a public speaking book that integrates content, design, and delivery. And, finally, I want to read a public speaking book steeped in the principles of storytelling, the most in-demand skill in business today.

I have wondered why this sort of book does not already exist – or at least why I have yet to find one. Here is the best explanation I could conceive: In contrast to a multitude of keynotes readily accessible on YouTube, examples of exceptional business presentations, especially ones that are legal to reproduce, are nearly impossible to find in the public domain. For instance, legend has it that Steve Jobs, upon his return to Apple in 1997, went to a whiteboard and drew a simple two-by-two grid. The rows were labeled "Desktop" and "Portable" and the columns "Consumer" and

"Professional." That meeting transformed a company suffering under the crushing weight of over 300 products. The underlying philosophy of minimalism now defines everything the company does. Since that meeting was not recorded, we have no idea who was in the room, how the meeting was structured, or how people interacted. Those types of meetings are highly confidential and companies only talk about them (with rose colored glasses) years later, if ever.

Besides geeking-out on public speaking for the past two decades, I have also worked my way up the ladder to become a senior executive in a company with nearly $2 billion in revenue; I craft and I critique high-stakes business presentations every day. Since I cannot release my employer's material, non-public presentations, I considered a few options when I decided to author this book. First, I tried to write a fictionalized tale of a new product manager introducing an electronic healthcare device in the business parable style of Patrick Lencioni's "The Five Dysfunctions of a Team" or Eliyahu Goldratt's "The Goal." However, I found myself repeatedly violating the storytelling maxim that exposition should always be the subtext of interaction between characters and never straight explanation. Fiction, or at least my fiction, was simply too contrived and inefficient to explore persuasive business storytelling.

When that attempt failed, I asked myself: Where do the most compelling strategy presentations come from? The answer, of course, is from top tier management consulting firms. I struck gold when I realized that these firms are often required to release their presentations when they serve public institutions. The gold mine turned to a diamond mine when I found an engagement that involved not one, but three of the top ten consulting firms – McKinsey & Company, The Boston Consulting Group, and Accenture.

In Section 1 of this book, I deconstruct the best-practice narrative frameworks each of the consulting firms followed to persuade their audiences. In Section 2, I extract world-class techniques for data-driven slide design. Finally, in Section 3, I cover verbal and non-verbal delivery principles that convey authority and authenticity in business settings.

With this backdrop, let's get started.

Chapter 1

The Perfect Storm

Sometime during the evening of January 26, 2009, a light freezing drizzle began to fall in central Kentucky. Over the course of the next two days, as the storm's reach broadened across the state, the drizzle turned to rain, the rain to sleet, the sleet to snow, and the snow to ice. When the storm was over, 609,000 homes and businesses were left without power and 35 Kentucky residents had lost their lives. [1] [2]

Among the towns hardest hit was tiny Lowes, Kentucky which lost telephone, Internet, and electricity service for three weeks. Supporting a population of merely 98 residents, Postmaster JoAnn Bell and her Postmaster Relief Becky Goin understandably could have suspended mail delivery service to tend to their own urgent needs. After all, more than 200 Post Offices were impacted across Kentucky. However, Joann and Becky kept their 137-year-old post office running by relying on very old-school technology including a vintage fan scale, a battery-powered adding machine, and an old-fashioned gas stove.[3] I can only imagine they were chanting the unofficial United States Postal Service creed – "Neither snow nor rain nor heat nor gloom of night stays these couriers from the swift

---

[1] http://www.crh.noaa.gov/lmk/?n=jan_2009_ice_and_snow
[2] http://en.wikipedia.org/wiki/January_2009_Central_Plains_and_Midwest_ice_storm
[3] http://about.usps.com/news/state-releases/ky/2009/ky_2009_0313.htm

completion of their appointed rounds" – in their minds as they skated their way through their delivery routes.

As the 2009 ice storm released its grip on the Central Plains and Midwestern United States, a perfect storm was forming that would affect all 36,496 retail post offices with their 623,128 employees.[4] Some of the clouds on the horizon had been visible as macro-trends for years. The double whammy of an aging workforce and increased healthcare costs was putting a burden on retirement obligations. Additionally, the Internet had long since relegated the traditional mailbox to a repository for junk mail, bills, and birthday cards.

The anvil that broke the camel's back –deep economic recession – could not have been predicted. After years of increases, volume dropped by 25 billion pieces of mail in 2009, resulting in a nearly 10 percent decline in revenue. Despite pursuing aggressive cost-cutting measures, the organization posted a net loss of just under $4 billion.

No stranger to outsourcing, the United States Postal Service turned to strategy consulting firms. In exchange for a reported $4.8 million[5], Accenture, The Boston Consulting Group (BCG), and McKinsey & Company (McKinsey) each examined a different part of the problem. BCG began by building a model to project mail volumes through 2020. Using the BCG model as an input, McKinsey crafted a set of strategic recommendations for the USPS mail business. In parallel, Accenture explored the possibility of

---

[4]https://about.usps.com/who-we-are/postal-facts/decade-of-facts-and-figures.htm
[5]http://money.cnn.com/2010/03/02/news/economy/usps/

diversification into non-mail products and services to improve USPS profitability.

You might expect the remainder of this book to follow a chronological progression from BCG to McKinsey to Accenture. That approach would be ideal if my objective were to reveal the development of the USPS business strategy. However, the USPS strategy is merely the vehicle to help you understand the best practices (and lessons to avoid) for creating persuasive, data-driven business presentations. In service of that objective, I will start with the McKinsey presentation since it is, in my opinion, the one that best exemplifies a strategic storytelling model.

Section 1:
Persuasive Content

Chapter 2

The Situation-Complication-Resolution Framework

Among top-tier consulting firms, McKinsey is broadly regarded as best-in-class at constructing persuasive business presentations. The firm's maniacal focus on presentation structure can be traced to one exceptional storyteller – Barbara Minto.

Barbara Minto has many path-paving firsts to her name. After working as a secretary at a railway company in the 1950s, Ms. Minto grew increasingly concerned about her job prospects as her boss aged into his 70s. In response, she applied and was among the first eight women accepted into Harvard Business School when it opened its doors to coeds in 1961. Upon graduation two years later, she became the first female consultant hired by McKinsey & Company. In her ten years at McKinsey, she developed her 'Pyramid Principle' for logically structuring consulting recommendations. Since 1973, she has run an independent communications training and consulting firm of her own, Minto International.

Ms. Minto's incredibly valuable contribution to effective business communications involved the novel synthesis of a number of frameworks from other disciplines. At the risk of extreme oversimplification, I'll attempt to summarize the precursors to her ideas and memorable takeaways from her work in a few short paragraphs.

First, she translated elements of the scientific method including hypothesis testing, inductive logic, and deductive logic into business-centric thinking. Ms. Minto advocates inductive logic for most problem-solving exercises, stressing the importance of considering mutually-exclusive and collectively exhaustive (MECE) sets of ideas.

Second, she combined the military's bottom-line-up-front (BLUF) technique with journalism's inverted pyramid narrative style to create a top-down approach to business-centric writing.

Third, and the thing for which she is most well-known, Ms. Minto recast 19th century German playwright Gustav Freytag's dramatic story arc into the situation-complication-question-answer (SCQA) approach to drafting introductions to business communications. (Commentators who have not closely read The Pyramid Principle mistakenly refer to SCQA and the Minto Pyramid Principle as one and the same.) In my opinion, Freytag's exposition is Minto's situation; Freytag's rising action is Minto's complication; Freytag's climax is Minto's question; and, Freytag's falling action and denouement are Minto's answer. Of course, even Freytag stands on the shoulders of giants, dating at least back to Aristotle's three-part structure (protasis, epitasis, and catastrophe – or more accessibly, beginning, middle, and end) as described in his Poetics.

Again, Ms. Minto applied her SCQA framework to creating structured, concise, and compelling introductions to written communications – especially memos and reports. In story parlance, the situation describes the recent context of "Once upon a time… and every day…" The complication includes the inciting incident and its consequences or "… until one day… and because of that…" The question captures the most intense query raised in a reader's mind in response to the complication – often "why?" or "how?" Note the question is often implied and therefore not typically written into the introduction. Finally, the answer offers a solution to the problem set up by the situation and complication inclusive of the climax and the aftermath, or "… until finally... and after that…"

As presentations replaced memos and reports, something curious happened to Minto's SCQA framework. Instead of being used only to craft introductions, the framework became the organizing principle for entire presentations. Since the question was "silent," it got dropped. In addition, the term "answer" was swapped with its synonym, "resolution." The resulting situation-complication-resolution (SCR) not only has a memorable rhyme to it, but also conforms to a beautiful three-act narrative structure.

To the best of my knowledge, Barbara Minto was not directly involved in the USPS engagement. However, the DNA of Ms. Minto's set of pyramid principle frameworks are readily apparent in McKinsey's presentation.

Before I show you any slides from their USPS engagement, I need to digress in order to show you how McKinsey consultants visualize problem solving using storyboarding techniques. This will take a little while, but I promise it will be worth your time.

Tip 1: Define the problem and make sure it is worth solving

Imagine you are a McKinsey partner and the Postmaster General of the United States approaches you and asks, "Can you help us reverse our drop in efficiency as measured by pieces of mail delivered per full-time-equivalent?" Before saying yes or no, you must take some time to define the problem and to make sure it is worth solving.

Validate whether the problem as initially stated is framed at the appropriate level. To move up, repeatedly ask what impact a problem has and then assess whether the impact is one that can be addressed by the client's key decision maker.

At USPS, for example, the impact of low delivery efficiency is high workforce cost - certainly within the remit of the Postmaster General. Continuing, high workforce cost is one component of high total cost – also within the control of the key decision maker. High total cost results in low profitability – still the Postmaster General's responsibility. Catastrophic losses at the USPS could lead to rising national debt accompanied by a drop in the credit rating of the federal government. That final increase in the scope of impact is one step too far, since the President and Congress, not the Postmaster

General, are accountable for the nation's credit rating. As this example illustrates, the only way to know if you have gone high enough is to push yourself one step too far and then come back. If your path leads you to the total annihilation of the known universe, so be it.

The McKinsey terminology for this process of problem scoping is called "moving up the issue tree." Issue trees can be visualized as outlines (see Figure 2-1) or as hierarchical graphs (see Figure 2-2). As the figures illustrate, associates are encouraged to express issues as questions in full sentence form, since doing so encourages clear thought and facilitates clear communication.

Although I posed all the issues in this example as "How...?" questions, best practice allows for any open-ended question. "How...?" questions tend to be the most common since the answers offer solutions in the form of steps or methods. "Why…" questions are the next most common since the answers explain root causes. Though "What…?", "Who…?", "When…?", and "Where…?" are rare, use them if appropriate.

> I. How can we improve profitability?
>   A. How can we lower total cost?
>   a. How can we lower workforce cost?
>   i. How can we improve our delivery efficiency?
>   ii. ...
>   b. ...
>   B. ...

Figure 2-1: Partial USPS issue tree in outline form

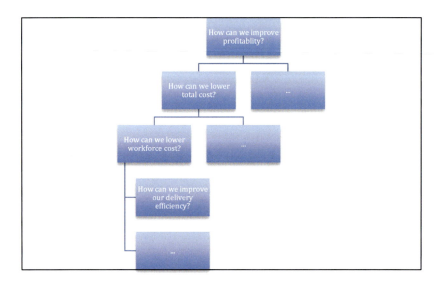

Figure 2-2: Partial USPS issue tree in hierarchical graph form

Tip 2: Identify constraints

In addition to validating whether or not the problem is scoped at the appropriate level, articulate the more traditional components of scope including constraints (also known as "guiding principles" to those who prefer a more positive spin.) Constraints may be organizational, but appear in other forms such as financial, environmental, regulatory, etc.

The USPS has the following three interlinked constraints governing what the organization is able to do without seriously impacting its core mission:

1. Universal Service Obligation (USO): The USO obligates the USPS to provide universal service at affordable prices and is "broadly outlined in multiple statutes and encompasses multiple dimensions: geographic scope, range of products, access to services and facilities, delivery frequency, affordable and uniform pricing, service quality, and security of the mail."[6]

2. Private Express Statutes (PES): This group of laws gives the USPS a monopoly on carrying letters for compensation. Letters are defined as messages directed to a specific person or address recording on a tangible object. The PES allows for the

---

[6] http://about.usps.com/universal-postal-service/usps-uso-executive-summary.pdf

existence of private carriers as long as they abide by anti-competitive exceptions such as requiring senders pay at least six times the price charged for a one-ounce First-Class letter.
3. Mailbox Access Rule: This rule states that mailboxes can only be used for the receipt of postage-paid mail delivered by USPS personnel.

These constraints rule out certain solutions such as selling access to mailboxes to private couriers, limiting delivery frequency in selected geographical areas, or selling alcohol or tobacco products.

Tip 3: Build out the mutually exclusive and collectively exhaustive set of issues

It may be that delivery efficiency is the best lever the Postmaster General has to improve the profitability of the USPS. However, you cannot be sure until you flesh out the issue tree by filling in the mutually exclusive and collectively exhaustive (MECE: *pronounced 'me-see'*) set of issues. Mutually exclusive means the issues are independent of each other. In my experience, issues sometimes mildly overlap, so do not get overly hung-up on perfection. Collectively exhaustive means all possible issues are included.

The McKinsey best practice for filling out an issue tree is to fully complete each level (outside-in for outline form; top-down for hierarchical graph form) before going deeper. Though the hierarchical graph form is prettier, I use the faster outline form.

In the USPS example, we have the top-level key issue of profitability defined. The next step is to explore what other factors at the same general level as total cost are as important in their impact on profit. There is just one mutually exclusive option – total revenue. Going a level deeper, the components of total cost include: workforce costs, retiree benefit costs, capital asset costs, etc. Staying at the same level, the drivers of total revenue include traditional mail revenue and non-traditional revenue.

How broad and how deep should you go? There is neither a single answer to the ideal number of issues per level nor a single answer to the ideal number of levels. The limiting factor on most consulting engagements is a set of time constraints, including: the overall project deadline, a contracted quantity of billable hours, and scheduled (often weekly) meetings with the client. Working backward, the project planner will set an allocation for the number of hours devoted to creating an issue tree. You simply rack your brain as much as you can in the time you have available. An issue tree is an amazing and highly efficient tool for uncovering what matters so you can get a lot done in very little time. If the team includes a consultant or client member with deep knowledge or prior experience with the same problem, high-impact issue trees can be constructed with blazing speed.

Tip 4: Convert your issue tree into a hypothesis tree

Within one day to one week of an engagement kickoff, first-time McKinsey clients are often startled when the consulting team shows up with what looks like a full set of solutions to the issues that were just uncovered. They object, "I paid you how much?! And you whiz-kids already think you have all the answers when you haven't even taken the time to do any real investigation?!"

What appears to be a set of solutions is merely a set of initial hypotheses, proposed explanations that now must be rigorously tested. A good problem solver will search for facts, all the while updating the hypothesis. Great problem solvers not only seek information that confirms their hypothesis but also mercilessly hunt for disconfirming information.

In statistics, a hypothesis can never be accepted. Rather, your only options are to either reject or fail-to-reject the hypothesis. Statistics loves uncertainty and this treatment of testing your hypotheses leaves an air of mystery. When you think about it, decisions in your personal or professional life are pretty much that way, too. You can never know with absolute certainty that you are making the right or best decision; you do the best you can with the information you have at the time.

A hypothesis tree is a set of decisive answers, represented in outline or hierarchical form, to the issue tree questions. "How can we improve profitability?" becomes "We can improve profitability by …"; "How can we lower total cost" becomes "We can lower total cost by …"; and so on. To ensure your hypotheses are testable, make them SMART just as we did with the overall presentation title in Chapter 2. (So that you do not need to page back, SMART stands for specific, measureable, action-oriented, relevant, and time-bound.)

Tip 5: Prioritize your hypotheses for impact

The process of constructing an issue tree and of subsequently converting it to a hypothesis tree is an efficient form of brainstorming. As such, each mutually exclusive and collectively exhaustive level should be developed in a judgment-free manner.

At this stage, the team working on the engagement is going to have to do a lot of work in a (usually) limited amount of time. Given the ultimate goal is to have the largest positive impact on the client's business, you must prioritize your hypotheses. When, not if, you run out of time, you can rest knowing your efforts were efficiently spent.

During your first pass at prioritization, gut feel or back-of-the-envelope calculations are sufficient as you will have few facts from which to draw. McKinsey assists its consultants by giving them the following guidance in such situations:

When prioritizing, it is common to use a two-by-two matrix – e.g. a matrix featuring "impact" and "ease of impact" as the two axes. Our focus on client impact makes it extremely likely that impact will form part of any prioritization. Other prioritization criteria include urgency (but beware the danger of being drawn into firefighting), fit with values and mission, strategic alignment, fit with capabilities, and option value. Applying some of these prioritization criteria will knock out portions of the issue tree altogether. Consider testing the issues against them all, albeit quickly, to help drive the prioritization process.[7]

As we go through the remainder of the USPS presentation, we will see how McKinsey prioritized solutions to the issues facing the organization.

Tip 6: "Ghost out" your story on paper using the situation-complication-resolution framework

The overwhelming majority of individuals responsible for developing presentations go directly to design tools such as PowerPoint or Keynote. While these software products are valuable, the great danger in using them too soon is that the resulting output is just a string of information.

McKinsey is very explicit that its associates "get to paper" quickly by building a rough draft known as a "ghost" deck. Although "paper" is a loose term, most of the firm's presentations really do begin as post-it notes, index cards, or full-sized pieces of paper divided into grids. Each page in a ghost deck includes a title at the top and the sketch of an exhibit, usually a graph or table, needed to prove the title in the body. Designing in this manner helps show the storyline that connects all the information together into a business narrative.

---

[7] Ian Davis, David Keeling, Paul Schreier, and Ashley Williams. "The McKinsey Approach to Problem Solving." A McKinsey published staff paper. 2007.

The dot-dash approach is a nice, electronic, McKinsey sanctioned design alternative to storyboarding with pen and paper. In a dot-dash outline, the storyline arguments are carried by dots (bullet points) and the supporting facts are sketched out with indented dashes (hyphens). For clarity, express the dots and the dashes in complete sentences. The dots become the slide titles and the dashes become the content in the body of the slide.

At a very high level, here is what the McKinsey USPS presentation looks like in dot-dash format: (Note: In a fully developed outline, the situation, complication, and resolution are expanded into many dots, and each dot may have many supporting dashes.)

- Situation: USPS is experiencing unprecedented losses
  - Profits in 2003 to 2006 have swung to steep losses in 2007 to 2010
- Complication: The "Base Case" leads to a loss of $33 billion and cumulative losses of $238 billion by 2020
  - Without action, unfavorable revenue and cost trends will continue
- Resolution: USPS must pursue fundamental change in five areas

- Change must occur in: Products & Services; Pricing; Service Levels; Workforce; and Public Policy

Tip 7: Test your hypotheses and iterate your story

Problem definition and the dot-dash approach mark the end of the first phase in developing a persuasive, data-driven presentation. This first phase must come before data collection and analysis because knowing the problem you are solving and the story you expect to tell guides you to what data to consider. While that may seem obvious, I find that most people jump to slicing and dicing data in a million ways to find things to say about it. Searching for problems and solutions in this way is like trying to find one fish in an ocean; there is simply too much information available inside and outside of most corporations.

The data used to test hypotheses can be drawn from a wide range of sources. In the USPS presentation, McKinsey primarily draws upon financial (e.g., net income) and operational (e.g., pieces of mail delivered) metrics. However, data can come from a wide range of external sources including competitors, suppliers, customers, as well as data aggregators such as governments and trade organizations.

When most people think of data, they think of quantitative statistics. However, McKinsey routinely draws upon qualitative data in its engagements and you should, too. While this is not a book on data collection techniques, there is one technique – bright spot analysis – that is so valuable I feel compelled to at least outline it for you here.

Bright spot analysis is designed to help you identify the best practice behaviors of the people who have successful outcomes. I'll illustrate by way of example.

Imagine you want to increase the average annual sales for individual account executives in your company by 25% from $100,000 to $125,000. An average leader working on this goal would come up with and apply some new ideas, perhaps even a best practice of a competitor. A better than average leader would inquire with a few trusted sales managers as to who their top performers are and then ask those account executives what they do to cultivate and close a prospect.

A great leader, one who applies bright spot analysis, does not trust sales managers to know who their top performers are. Yes, that is blasphemy, but sales managers are people too, and hold biases due to personal relationships and past performance. The right first step is to stack rank account executives by recent performance – for instance, sales over the last two quarters. Next, divide the list into four (quartiles) or five (quintiles) groups. Ensure the top group is well over the $125,000 sales goal to make sure there is existence-proof for what you are trying to achieve. Take the time to eliminate outliers in the top group who may have benefitted from special circumstances such as one massive transaction. Do the same for the bottom group, again eliminating account executives that suffered due to uncontrollable circumstances.

Now go out and interview the top ten performers. Rather than asking them what they do or what they would do in the abstract, apply an anthropological approach by asking them to walk you step-by-step through a recent transaction they completed. How did they first identify the prospect? How did they make first contact? What resources did they bring to bear during the sales process? Who was involved in the decision? How did they close the transaction? As you interview multiple people, you will start to hear patterns. Rather than asking the ineffective question, "What are your best practices?" you are discovering best practices by listening for behaviors common among successful people.

Most bright spot analyses stop there. However, the best go through the exact same anthropological interview processes with the bottom performers. That step is critical because bright spots are behaviors top performers apply that bottom performers do not. Once you find the delta, you can teach everyone what your top performers are doing and maybe even blow way past your goal of a 25% improvement.

Keep in mind the tremendous potential for bias tied to knowing ahead of time which interviewees are top- and bottom-performers. To mitigate that bias, strive to ask open-ended, non-leading questions and spend the vast majority of the conversation as a listener.

* * * * *

For the sake of simplicity, I have made it seem as though the process of generating and then iterating on a storyboard using problem-solving techniques is linear. In real engagements, consultants move back-and-forth between problem definition, issue trees, hypothesis trees, and storyboards as they gather and synthesize new information.

Also for the sake of simplicity, I have implied that this process is fully your responsibility or the responsibility of your group. McKinsey strives to engage clients in co-creation to ensure the best solutions are uncovered and to secure buy-in for the resulting change needed to turn recommendations into action.

This chapter established the core problem solving and storyboarding techniques used to develop persuasive, fact-based presentations. Now, let us dive into McKinsey's USPS engagement, picking up at the first part of its situation-complication-resolution story.

Chapter 3

McKinsey's USPS Situation

The situation-complication-resolution (SCR) storytelling framework requires only that each of the three components exist in the narrative. However, presenters can begin their stories with any one of the three in order to affect the emotions of their audiences.

When listeners are extremely anxious, begin with the resolution. This is known in military parlance as 'bottom-line-up-front" (BLUF) and in consulting terminology as starting with the top of the inverted pyramid. For this approach to have a soothing effect, you must be reasonably certain your audience will easily understand and readily accept your recommendation as a compelling solution to its problem. If not, you may end up doing more harm than good. Furthermore, giving away the ending at the beginning kills all dramatic tension and makes for an extremely boring presentation. Due to the risk of either extreme tension or zero tension, starting a presentation with a resolution should be reserved for rare circumstances.

If your audience is overly complacent, begin with the complication to create a sense of urgency. In dramatic storytelling, this would be like starting an action movie in the middle of an intense car chase or at the moment the hero jumps off a cliff and into a helicopter in the nick of time. In typical business meetings, decision makers are not complacent. Therefore, it is unwise to increase their tension too quickly at the beginning of your presentation.

If starting with the resolution introduces (typically) too little tension and starting with the complication introduces too much, starting with the situation is just right. The situation addresses the question, "What is going on and how did we get here?" Because it provides critical context, this is the conventional way of beginning a strategic story and is the way McKinsey began its USPS presentation.

Tip 8: Title your presentation with a "so-what" encapsulating your overall objective

McKinsey chose a rather bland "what" title, "USPS Future Business Model" for its presentation as shown in slide #0 (Figure 3-1). "What" titles, technically noun phrases, lack the audience-focused emotional punch you find in "so-what" titles describing outcomes. First and foremost, titles must orient your listeners to your overall objective. Frankly, I am surprised this title slipped through McKinsey's tight quality control.

If you search the web carefully, you will notice consistency in the way McKinsey titles its presentations. For instance, "Sustaining Quality and Operational Excellence," "Capturing the Full Electricity Efficiency Potential of the U.K.," and "Evolving USSA's Alpine Domestic Development System in Partnership with Clubs." Notice all three examples begin with a powerful –ing verb. This verb form, the present participle, is used to describe action that is still taking place.

Among the three consulting firms participating in the USPS engagement, McKinsey had the juiciest piece – recommending a high-level strategy to restore the postal service to profitability. Had the firm used its own best practice, they might have titled this presentation, "Evolving the USPS Future Business Model." Using a variety of other verbs at the beginning such as optimizing, designing, or transforming would have been equally effective.

Occasionally, you will find a McKinsey presentation with other types of titles. The most common alternative to the "so-what" title is the question title. For instance, the McKinsey presentation entitled, "Quantum Leap – What Will It Take to Double Serbia's Economic Growth in the Next Decade?" I think better editors would have dropped the flowery "quantum leap" and turned the question into the more direct, "Doubling Serbia's Economic Growth in the Next Decade."

Another unusual (for McKinsey) example I found was entitled, "How Companies Can Capture the Veteran Opportunity." Again, a good editor would boil this down to "Capturing the Veteran Opportunity."

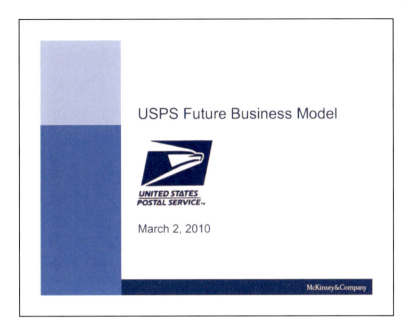

Figure 3-1: McKinsey's USPS presentation slide #0

Tip 9: Make your presentation title SMART

On the off chance that you have not come across the SMART framework in any of the countless books on personal or professional goal setting, here is a quick refresher. SMART goals are specific, measurable, action-oriented, relevant, and time-bound. McKinsey teaches its associates to evaluate their overall objective, sometimes referred to as the basic question to be resolved, using this framework. Consequently, best-practice presentation titles are SMART.

As an example, consider again, "Doubling Serbia's Economic Growth in the Next Decade." It is specific in its reference to Serbia's economic growth. It is measurable in its reference to doubling. It is action-oriented, an attribute that comes for free when you use a powerful –ing verb. Relevancy is audience depending, but we can assume McKinsey created that presentation for Serbian officials or another interested party such as the World Bank. It is time-bound in its reference to "the next decade."

An important side note is that the "A" and the "R" in the SMART framework are sometimes represented as "accountable" and "reasonable." Accountability is often implied but can be made explicit by mentioning the party responsible for achieving the goal in the title. Similarly, reasonableness is implicit and in the eye of the beholder. Because of this fuzziness, action-oriented and relevant make better checklist items.

So, how could McKinsey have made its USPS title SMART? In some ways, they were a little stuck because the overall USPS project was called the "USPS Future Business Model." However, if they had more flexibility they could have used, "Restoring the USPS to Profitability by 2020," which was, as we will discover, the ultimate goal of this presentation.

Tip 10: Use an agenda slide to provide your audience with a roadmap

In dramatic storytelling, plots are designed to include long stretches of rising tension. To build emotional intensity, writers keep their audiences guessing with delayed resolutions to questions such as, "What is going to happen next?" While strategic storytelling has tension, business presentation designers strive to keep tension short lived because their goal is persuasion.

Showing an agenda slide immediately after your title slide is one of the best ways to control tension. First, audiences expect it. Second, by knowing where you are going, they are more likely to hold questions until relevant sections.

Tip 11: Keep agenda slide titles short and sweet so they can be ignored

There are several elements to notice about McKinsey's agenda slide shown in slide #1 (Figure 3-2), beginning with the slide title, also known as the slide lead. As in this presentation, the firm appears to have standardized on "Contents," though one can find two variations. The most common is "Agenda," which I find more appropriate when referring to a roadmap that will be delivered live rather than read passively. The other variation I have found is an agenda slide title that echoes the overall presentation title. For example, in the McKinsey presentation entitled, "Achieving Sustainable Development in Mining," the agenda slide title reads "Sustainable Development in Mining." In the case agenda slide titles, a degree of flexibility is appropriate. Unlike titles for content slides, titles for agenda slides should be unobtrusive since the audience's focus should be on the body of the slide. To that end, keep agenda slide titles short and sweet so they can be visually ignored. In theory, you could even do away with the agenda title altogether, though that is not something you see in McKinsey presentations.

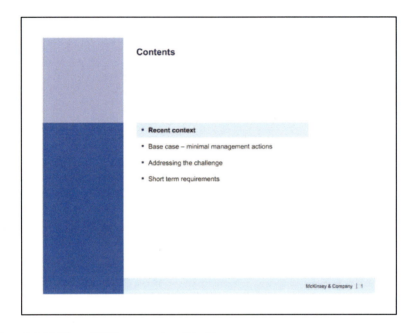

Figure 3-2: McKinsey USPS presentation slide #1

Tip 12: Limit agendas to no more than five short items

The set of bullets that comprise the body of the agenda slide is the next element to notice. Most McKinsey presentations I have seen have "three plus one" agenda items. Why not just say "four?" The reason is that the first three bullets encompass the full narrative of the story. The first bullet is the situational background, referred to in the USPS agenda slide as "Recent Context." The second bullet is the complication, referred to in the USPS agenda slide as "Base case – minimal management actions." The third bullet is the recommended strategy to solve the complication(s), referred to in the USPS presentation as "Addressing the challenge." Finally, in most McKinsey presentations, the "plus one" is labeled "Appendix." In the case of the USPS presentation, as we will explore later, the engagement team elevated the Appendix to higher priority because of a burning recommendation they found that was outside the context of the 2020 strategy.

Of course, you likely already noticed the bullets in the McKinsey USPS agenda slide are extremely short – at most five words. Moreover, there are no sub-bullets. While I have seen the rare McKinsey agenda slide violate the single line agenda item rule, I have yet to see the no sub-bullet rule violated. The reason for this simplicity is that the purpose of agenda slides is merely to guide the narrative flow, not to impart information. To that end, you will rarely find footnotes or graphical adornments on a McKinsey agenda slide.

Tip 13: Add creativity to agenda slide design

There is no rule requiring agenda items appear as numbered or bulleted text. If your presentation, like most strategic stories, is structured hierarchically, consider representing the agenda using an organizational chart. Similarly, if your presentation unfolds linearly, jazz it up by converting bulleted text to process chevrons. Finally, you can get even more creative with graphical agenda slides.

Tip 14: Start agenda items with action verbs to signal in which mental mode you want your audience

In McKinsey agenda slides, I have rarely seen parallel construction applied to bullet items in which each phrase or clause has the same grammatical structure. As I am somewhat of a stickler for grammar, this choice has always puzzled me. When I design agenda slides, I always apply parallelism. In particular, I start agenda bullets with action verbs. In each section of a presentation, I find it best to let my audience know in which mode it is.

Executives, being executives, have a natural prioritization of how best to use their time and brains during meetings. Unless told otherwise, their default mode is decision making. When I want the people I am presenting to in that mode, I start my bullet with "Approve…," "Adopt…," or "Authorize…" The second mode executives operate in is problem-solving mode. If you start a bullet with "Problem solve…," "Explore…," or "Brainstorm…," your audience knows you are seeking thoughtful input rather than a quick decision. Finally, the third mode in which executives operate is the passive listening one. Spend the least time in this final mode because it is not an effective use of senior leaders' time. I begin agenda bullets with "Review…" or "Evaluate…" to signal to my audience that I am about to share information.

Given this set of best practices, I would rewrite the agenda items as follows:

- Review USPS operating environment
- Evaluate 2020 base case assuming minimal action
- Approve recommendations to restore profitability
- Secure short-term financing to maintain solvency

It is perfectly acceptable to use the same action verb at the beginning of multiple bullets. At their core, business presentations are about clarity and efficiency, not literary excellence.

Tip 15: Apply contrast to highlight the start of each agenda section

The McKinsey standard for highlighting the start of each agenda section combines bold, black text and a colored, usually blue, box as reflected in slide #1 (Figure 3-2). I find that using one, or at most two, treatments to draw out contrast is sufficient. Adding others, such as different text color, underlining, or italics is overkill and may appear amateurish.

A presenter has two options for delivering this agenda slide. The short-form option is: "Let's begin with the recent context" followed by an extended pause to allow the audience to read the remainder of the roadmap. While that approach is perfectly fine, many presenters will be uncomfortable with the required silence and will opt for a long-form approach as follows: "Today, we'll review the recent context describing the past and current profitability of the USPS. Next, we'll explore the base forecast for profitability assuming minimal actions are taken to stem projected losses. Then, we'll propose a set of recommendations to address the challenges we face. Finally, although not part of our long-term strategy mandate, we'd like to share a key short-term finding with you. Now, let's begin with the recent context." This long-form version has a bit of embellishment around the bullets but does not, and should not, reveal too much content nor trigger too much tension.

Tip 16 : Start the situation with the current state of the fundamental issue

I find starting a business presentation is often the hardest part of the strategic storytelling process. To make the job easier, I follow a few simple rules. First, the beginning must frame the current state, including relevant history, of the fundamental issue. Second, the beginning should rely on facts drawn from internal or external information sources. Third, the beginning should be uncontroversial in the sense that your audience already knows the information, or at least can be assumed to have a sense of it.

The beginning of a business presentation should orient the audience and not trigger strong objections. Note that just because something is factual and uncontroversial does not mean it is emotionally neutral. In fact, you want a mild degree of tension to hook your audience from the start.

McKinsey's first situation slide (Figure 3-3) meets all three of these rules. Recall that a mounting financial loss was the fundamental problem facing the USPS. To illustrate this issue, McKinsey wisely chose to show the trend in net profits and losses for the organization. The mounting losses, although emotionally negative, were factual and readily known by the audience.

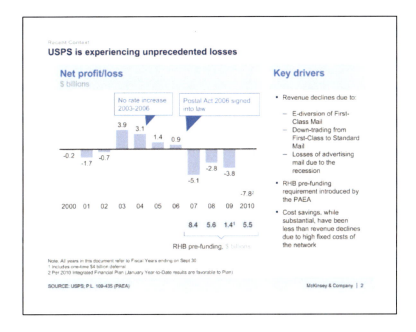

Figure 3-3: McKinsey's USPS presentation slide #2

Tip 17: To "own the flow," each slide should trigger a question answered by the title of the next slide

When you read the title "USPS is experiencing unprecedented losses" in slide #2 (Figure 3-3), what question naturally comes to mind? For me, as I suspect it is for most people, the question is "Why are unprecedented losses occurring?" or equivalently, "What are the root causes of the losses?"

While I might have chosen to answer this question on the next slide, Figure x actually provides three answers in the "Key drivers" text panel. First, revenues declined due to a number of factors. Second, non-operating costs to fund retirement health benefits (RHB) have been a major factor since the Postal Accountability and Enhancement Act of 2006 (PAEA) was signed into law. Third, operating cost savings has been insufficient.

The next question that arises is, "What impact has each of these three key drivers had on the mounting losses?" The McKinsey team answers that on slide #3 (Figure 3-4), entitled, "Losses have been driven by volume declines, RHB pre-funding requirements, and limitations on cost savings." The waterfall chart on the slide illustrates the impact of each of the three root causes on the decline in net income in 2009 as compared to 2006.

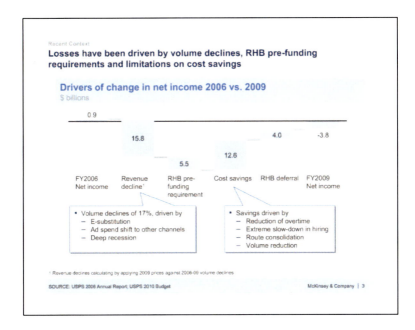

Figure 3-4: McKinsey's USPS presentation slide #3

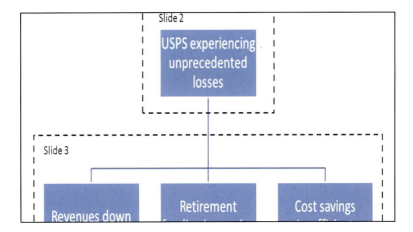

Figure 3-5: McKinsey USPS situation through slide 3

Figure 3-5 show the situation part of the strategic story evolving hierarchically. Slide 2 triggers a "Why...?" question that is answered by a set of reasons, or root causes, on slide 3. Importantly, each item is part of a mutually-exclusive and collectively-exhaustive set summarizing at a high-level everything else to follow in the situation.

Barbara Minto refers to the enumeration in slide #3 (Figure 3-4) as a "key line." I'll use the term "summary node" which is more descriptive and more consistent with the tree-traversal process we will explore in the next tip. Nearly every presentation has a summary node as either the first or second in each of the situation, complication, and resolution sections; in addition, many presentations have additional summary slides within sections to introduce new groups of idea.

Tip 18: Expand on the summary node with depth-first tree traversal

To understand how to sequence the remaining situation slides as you expand on the root causes identified in slide #3 (Figure 3-4), let's turn briefly to the concept of tree-traversal from computer science. Don't worry, I promise not to get too technical.

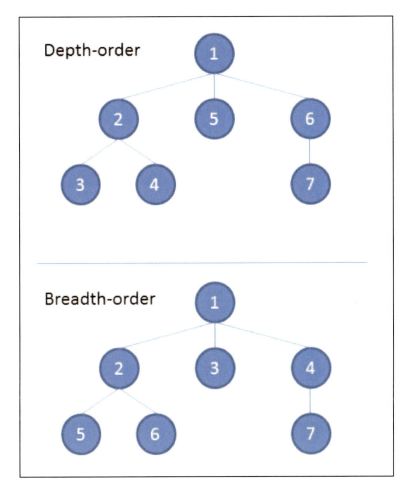

Figure 3-6: Depth-order and breadth-order tree traversal for the "Jane's Day" story

For starters, think of your presentation as a tree and each slide as a node in the tree. Tree traversal is simply the order in which you visit the nodes in the tree, or equivalently, the order in which you show slides in the presentation.

Brilliant minds figured out two basic methods for tree-traversal, including depth-first and breadth-first, as illustrated in Figure 3-6.

Traversal in either method begins with the root node, node #1. In depth-order tree traversal, any time you encounter multiple nodes at the same horizontal level, you go down first and only go across when you cannot go down any more. In breadth-order, any time you encounter multiple nodes at the same horizontal level, you go across first and only go down when you cannot go across anymore.

For presentations, use depth-first traversal since this method progressively introduces concepts and then "peels the onion." Additionally, this method more closely approximates how stories are told. This is painfully obvious when you consider telling a simple story of "Jane's Day" in each of the two ways as follows:

Depth-order: Jane woke up one morning and started her day (node #1). First, she ate breakfast (node #2). Her breakfast included coffee (node #3) and oatmeal (node #4). Next, she went to work (node #5). After work, she met her friend, Constance, at the park (node #6) and the two went for a run (node #7).

Breadth-order: Jane woke up one morning and started her day (node #1). First, she ate breakfast (node #2). Next, she went to work (node #3). After work, she met her friend Constance at the park (node #4). Back when she had breakfast, her breakfast included coffee (node #5) and oatmeal (node #6). Later, at the park after work, Jane and Constance went for a run (node #7).

Returning to McKinsey's USPS presentation, the root node of the situation is slide #2 (Figure 3-3) and its only child node is slide #3 (Figure 3-4), a summary node outlining three root causes.

Following the depth-first tree traversal method, the next slide must explore something having to do with revenue declines, but what? Once again, the content of the next slide is always the answer to the natural question triggered by the current slide. Audience members will want to know, "Why are revenues declining?"

The MECE set of root causes for declining mail revenues must consider changes in pricing and changes in volume, precisely the two factors explored in the next slide in the series, as shown in slide #4 (Figure 3-7). The slide thoroughly explains the pricing problem – the PAEA of 2006 limited increases by anchoring mail pricing to the Consumer Price Index (CPI). However, the slide only introduces the problem with mail volumes.

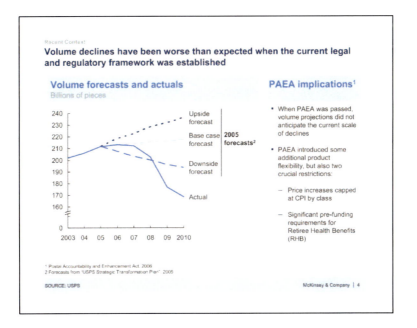

Figure 3-7: McKinsey's USPS presentation slide #4

To explain why actual mail volume in 2009 was significantly below even the downside forecast, we need to traverse one level deeper in the revenue decline part of the tree as shown in slide #5 (Figure 3-8). The shortfall is due to two factors. The first, economic recession, is reasonably well illustrated in the chart. The second, e-diversion (i.e. the inevitable switch from traditional mail to email and instant messaging), is mentioned only in the header and unfortunately not supported by proof in this or subsequent slides.

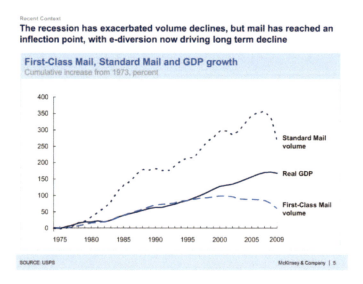

Figure 3-8: McKinsey's USPS presentation slide #5

Tip 19: Only go as deep as is needed to introduce the problem

With slide #5 (Figure 3-8), McKinsey went as deep as needed on the revenue part of the USPS situation. It is enough to know that price increases are capped and that volumes have been hampered by the recession and by e-diversion. In theory, one falls endlessly down the rabbit hole with increasing levels of granularity. Why is Standard mail, which previously had the fastest growth, collapsing so rapidly? And on… and on…

While there is no hard and fast rule on how many levels to go, I can offer a few guidelines. Go as deep as you need to introduce the problem. There is one successful outcome to a persuasive business presentation – the decision maker approves your recommendation. To that end, there is no need to show off your knowledge and your analytical prowess. In the situation, stop at the level of detail on which you intend to build in the complication and which you intend to rectify in your resolution. If you still want a rule with which to start, McKinsey often goes two levels deep – as they did in the revenue situation and will do in the third portion, the cost story, of the situation.

Tip 20: Repeat summary node slides when moving across after going deep

If you go very deep down a part of your tree, say three or more levels, you may want to repeat the summary node to help reorient your audience. In this example, that would mean repeating slide #3

(Figure 3-4) in order to smooth your transition across to the retirement health benefits situation (RHB). To change the focus, add visual emphasis to the "RHB pre-funding requirement" references in the slide.

In this case, perhaps since they only went two levels deep on revenue, McKinsey did not repeat the summary node slide when transitioning to the lone slide on pre-funding of retirement health benefits as shown in slide #6 (Figure 3-9).

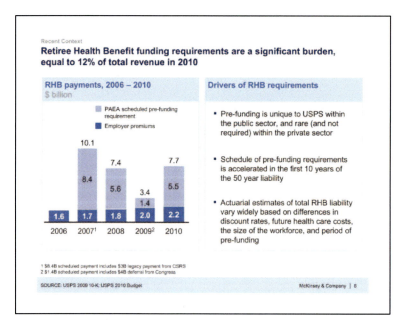

Figure 3-9: McKinsey's USPS presentation slide #6

As the summary node slide was not repeated in the transition to retiree health benefits, it was not repeated in the transition to the cost situation in slide #7 (Figure 3-10). In such cases, it is incredibly important that the slide title reorient the audience to where the speaker is in her story. Unfortunately, "Recent reductions in workforce usage have been significant, but pieces per FTE still declined in 2009" feels a little out of left field. The transitional flow would have been much smoother with a title referencing cost savings, as in: "Cost savings have been insufficient due to lower efficiency despite workforce reductions."

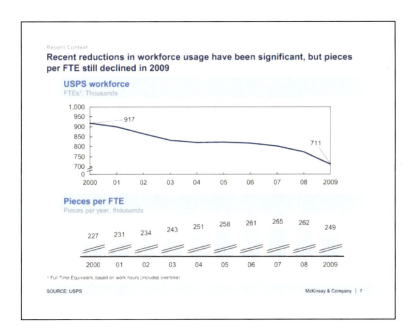

Figure 3-10: McKinsey's USPS presentation slide #7

Slide #7 (Figure 3-10) triggers the question, "Why didn't you reduce the workforce faster?" Slide #8 (Figure 3-11) provides the answer. The USPS did as much as it could by eliminating non-career employees and reducing overtime hours. Presumably, the next round of cuts must be deeper and, although not mentioned, would require painful contract negotiations with the powerful American Postal Workers Union (APWU), part of the even more powerful AFL-CIO.

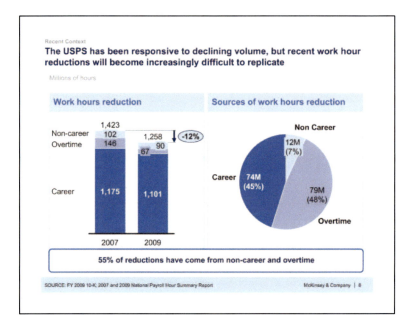

Figure 3-11: McKinsey's USPS presentation slide #8

* * * * *

We now have the complete context describing how the USPS found itself facing unprecedented losses. Figure 3-12 nicely summarizes the situation and also illustrates how the McKinsey team structured and sequenced this first act of the story. While it may be tempting to start thinking about ways to return the USPS to profitability, we must first develop a picture for what the future is likely to hold if no further action is taken.

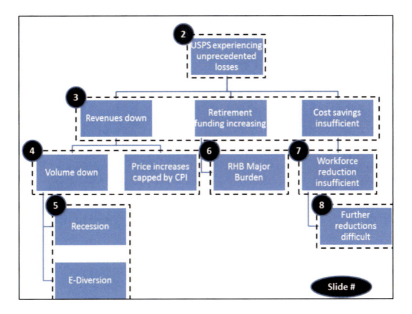

Figure 3-12: Full McKinsey USPS situation

Chapter 4

McKinsey's USPS Complication

Tip 21: Explore issues <u>and/or</u> opportunities in the complication section

McKinsey's situation section explored the historical fact-base leading to the USPS's profit predicament. The complication section, Act II of the strategic story, built tension in a controlled manner by focusing on current and future forces of change. Though the word "complication" carries a negative connotation, these forces of change can exacerbate problems or explore opportunities. In this case, the vast majority of the USPS complication section, introduced innocuously enough as "Base case – minimal management actions" in slide #9 (Figure 4-1), plays to negative emotions by escalating a predicament into a catastrophe.

Figure 4-1: McKinsey's USPS presentation (slide #9)

Tip 22: Build up to contentious or counter-intuitive insights

The USPS complication section deviates from the bottom-line up-front approach used in the situation section because the base case cumulative loss through 2020 is so extreme as to be contentious. As a result, the audience needs to be taken there through a build-up of information that resonates. If the base case were merely extreme but neither contentious nor counter-intuitive, then the complication should begin with the top-level forecast and then drill into the details.

Tip 23: Explore the influence of dynamic trends on the factors discussed in the situation

Recall that the situation ultimately deconstructed the levers driving USPS profitability into four components: the impact of volume on revenue, the impact of pricing on revenue, the impact of retirement health benefits on costs, and the impact of workforce efficiency on costs. As shown in slide #10 (Figure 4-2), the complication section starts by exploring the influence of dynamic trends on these same factors.

Figure 4-2: McKinsey's USPS presentation slide #10

Thinking in terms of story, profitability is the protagonist. The strategic business levers represent the protagonist's friends and foes.

All of these "characters" were introduced during Act I, the situation. Now, in Act II, the complication, we get to see characters with whom we are already familiar evolve through conflict in the form of trends. Shrewdly, many of these trends, such as e-Diversion and capped price increases, were already foreshadowed.

The limited amount of new information in slide #10 (Figure 4-2), a summary node, eases the audience into escalating tension following the now familiar depth-first tree traversal approach to slide order (see Figure 4-3).

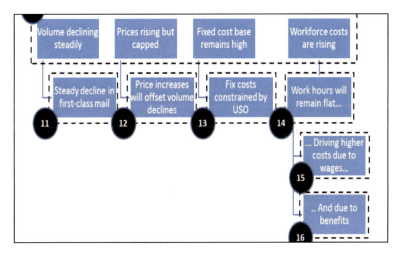

Figure 4-3: Beginning of USPS complication section expanding on four trends impacting revenues and costs

We already observed in the summary section that Standard-mail and First-Class-Mail volumes have been declining as a result of e-diversion and less advertising during the recession. Slide #11 (Figure 4-4) projects those negative trends forward in 2020.

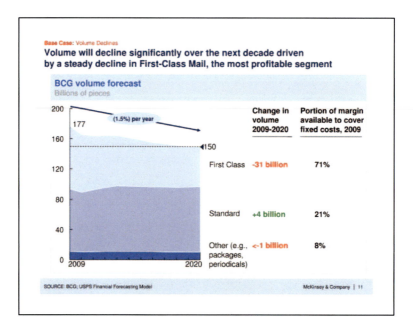

Figure 4-4: McKinsey's USPS presentation slide #11

Slide #12 (Figure 4-5) offers the one moderate piece of good news in the base case outlook for USPS profitability. Due to inflation-driven price increases, revenue will actually increase slightly despite the volume decline. From a story point of view, we move from negative (1.5% per year annual volume decline) to positive (0.16% per year annual revenue increase). However, like any good story, in Act II one step forward will soon be offset with two steps back.

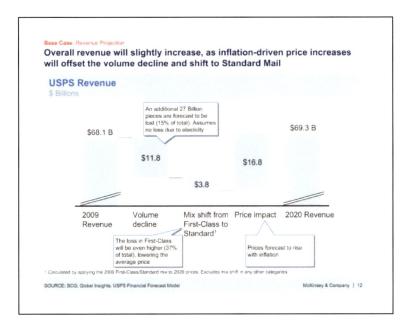

Figure 4-5: McKinsey's USPS presentation slide #12

Slide #13 (Figure 4-6) introduces the first part of the cost complication. The USPS is obligated to provide a universal standard of service to which Americans have become accustomed including access to post offices nearby and rapid delivery six days a week to nearly anywhere. These services rely heavily on fixed-cost capital (post-office buildings, sortation plants, and large vehicles); consequently, these costs will not fall as mail volume drops.

Figure 4-6: McKinsey's USPS presentation (slide #13)

The outlook grows darker still in slide #14 (Figure 4-7) as work hour savings from reduced mail volumes and fewer post offices are offset by work hour increases needed to deliver to additional locations.

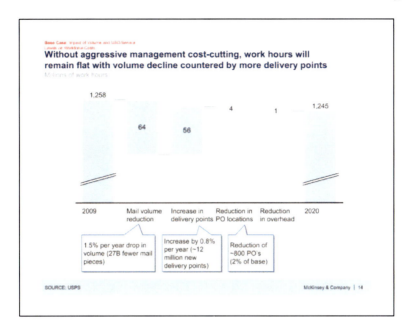

Figure 4-7: McKinsey's USPS presentation (slide #14)

Unfortunately, flat total work hours does not translate into flat workforce costs because wages, workers' comp, and health insurance are projected to increase much faster than inflation as shown in slide #15 (Figure 4-8).

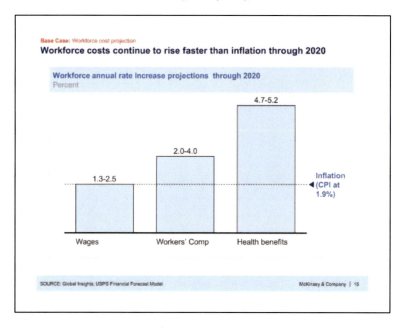

Figure 4-8: McKinsey's USPS presentation (slide #15)

On seeing slide #15 (Figure 4-8), an audience member's most natural question is likely, "Why are health benefits rising so much faster than inflation?" Slide #16 (Figure 4-9) reveals the root causes as a combination of pre-funding retiree health benefits and normal premiums for current employees.

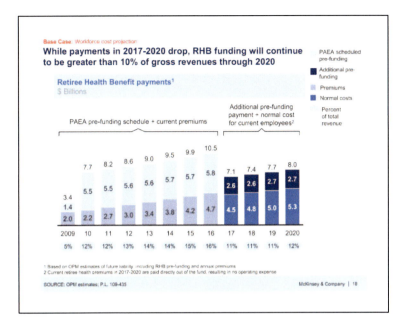

Figure 4-9: McKinsey's USPS presentation slide #16

Tip 24: Deliver the collective impact of the complications on the fundamental issue

At this point in the complication section of McKinsey's USPS presentation, we know the following: (1) despite volume declines, revenue will rise slightly as a result of price increases; (2) capital fixed costs will likely increase with the expansion in delivery points far surpassing the reduction in post offices; and, (3) variable wage and benefits costs, on a flat base of total hours, will likely increase faster than inflation.

So, revenues will rise slightly *and* costs will increase – probably more than slightly. But, we do not yet know by how much nor do we know the collective impact of these projections on profitability.

Now, it is time to put all the information together. Again, this build-up was slow because what is about to come is so dire it is shocking. In fact, it is so dire that the central complication will take three more slides to be fully clear.

First, slide #17 (Figure 4-10) combines all of the trends together into the revenue-impact and cost-impact *per piece of mail*. It feels reasonable that costs per piece will increase 4% per year and revenues per piece will increase 2% per year, given all of the similarly reasonable information disclosed thus far.

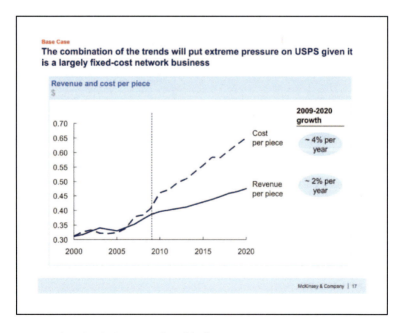

Figure 4-10: McKinsey's USPS presentation slide #17

Slide #18 (Figure 4-11) builds to the climax of the story, the end of Act II, in three parts. First, the chart on the left hand side multiplies the forecasted per-piece costs and revenues by projected volumes. Second, the middle chart subtracts the resulting total cost forecast from the total revenue forecast to create the net profit forecast. Notably, losses accelerate nearly every year, eventually hitting $33 billion! Of course, the forecast is highly sensitive to projected volume; nonetheless, the loss is a still shocking $21 billion, even in the unlikely event total mail volume remains flat. Third, the chart on the right hand side shows cumulative losses will reach $238 billion by 2020, fifteen times greater than the $15 billion statutory debt ceiling.

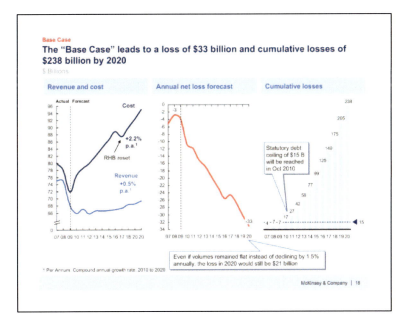

Figure 4-11: McKinsey's USPS presenation (slide #18)

Since slide #18 (Figure 4-11) proclaims catastrophe, some audience members will remain in disbelief. They might ask, "What were your critical assumptions and how certain are you about them?" Slide #19 (Figure 4-12) addresses this question and closes out the complication by exploring potential upside factors and potential downside risks. While not quantifying the impact of each of these, one can move the next part of the story, confident the $238 billion cumulative loss sits at a reasonable mid-point of a range of potential outcomes.

Figure 4-12: McKinsey's USPS presentation slide #19

* * * * *

Pause to think about the elegance of the storytelling in the complication section. The protagonist established in Act I, USPS profitability, was affected by friends and foes met during her journey through Act II. Notably, the story was tightly edited in the sense that every trend had a conclusive impact on either revenue or cost; the trends converged to the story's climactic moment, leaving the audience hungry to discover our hero's savior.

Just how accurate were McKinsey's projections? For 2010, the year already in progress when the presentation was given, the firm forecast a $10 billion loss versus an actual loss of $17.6 billion. After this larger than expected loss, the 2011 retirement health benefit payment was deferred into 2012. For 2011, the firm forecast a loss of $10 billion versus an actual loss of $8.7 billion. For 2012, the firm forecast a loss of $15 billion versus an actual loss of $30.7 billion. Finally, for 2013, the firm forecast a loss of $16 billion versus an actual loss of $11.6 billion. (Note: Actual losses include net operating loss, retirement health benefits pre-funding expenses, and workers' compensation expenses.)

Cumulatively from 2010 to 2013, McKinsey forecast a loss of $51 billion. The actual loss was $68.6 billion. Firms like McKinsey strive for plus or minus 10% accuracy. In this case, the actual loss was thirty-five percent worse than projected. At least as I type these words, the McKinsey forecast is, if anything, highly conservative. Said another way, the complication facing the United States Postal Service is truly catastrophic.

Here, at the end of Act II of our strategic story, our protagonist, USPS profitability, teeters precariously at the edge of a cliff. The recommendations the organization chooses to apply from the upcoming resolution section have existential consequences; in order to survive, the USPS needs to fundamentally change how it makes and spends money.

Chapter 5

McKinsey's USPS Resolution

As the agenda slide "curtain" (Figure 5-1) rises on the third and final act of McKinsey's USPS strategic story, let's take a moment to recap the action thus far. In Act I, the USPS – our hero – was struggling with financial losses stemming from e-Diversion, recession, retirement health benefit funding, and limited flexibility in reducing costs. In Act II, these forces were forecast to intensify, leading to a projected $238 billion cumulative loss by 2020. Even the glimmer of a way out, due to potential upside trends in the general economy, was tempered by equally strong potential downside risks. At this pivotal moment, the audience has one natural question, "How can the USPS get out of this mess?"

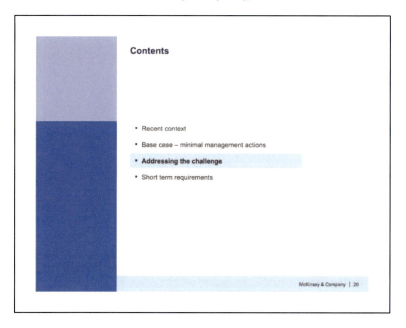

Figure 5-1: McKinsey's USPS presentation slide #20

Tip 25 : Explore the mutually exclusive and collectively exhaustive ways to resolve the complication

Generally, three levels of effort can be applied to solve any problem. The first level includes standard, low-risk actions taken as ordinary business process optimization. The second level includes radical, high-risk actions leading to fundamental innovation and change. The third level, one many decision makers fail to consider, is maintaining the status quo; the decision to "do nothing" is indeed a decision and can often be the best option.

Using these three levels of action as part of brainstorming opens up a wide range of possibilities. Here, I use the term brainstorming broadly to include sourcing and synthesizing ideas from internal and external sources either via observation or creative effort.

Tip 26: Place low-impact resolutions in the Appendix to show they have been considered but ruled out

As shown in slide #21 (Figure 5-2), the McKinsey team decided to include a set of standard actions and a set of radical actions. Rather unfortunately, the slide mixes two MECE ways of parsing the solution space. One way is standard versus fundamental change. The other way is actions within USPS control and actions outside of USPS control. Based on the remainder of the resolution section, the orange outlined text box labeled "Actions within Postal Service Control" should have read "Organic Change" or some other antonym of fundamental change.

Notably, the status quo future was already covered in the complication section, so it need not be repeated. Had the status quo "base case" not been presented, it should have been placed in the Appendix because a decision maker might ask about it, though it is not attractive enough as a recommended option.

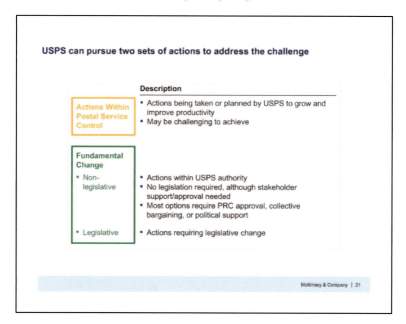

Figure 5-2: McKinsey's USPS presentation slide #21

Tip 27: Prioritize recommendations in impact-, sequential-, or emotional order

Once brainstorming is complete, the storyteller must prioritize in order to determine which ideas to put into the story and in which sequence. The decision makers in the audience not only are judging the quality of the solutions offered, but also are judging the quality of the person offering the ideas. If one includes too many low-impact ideas, one risks leaving the decision makers both overwhelmed with content and underwhelmed with confidence. Starting with low-impact ideas will similarly destroy decision maker confidence.

Choosing how to order actions in the resolution section is critically important. The default for prioritizing solutions is in descending order, highest to lowest, of impact since this releases the anxiety built at the end of the complication section as fast as possible. However, this default does not work when the actions must be taken in sequence (i.e., phased) or when the audience needs to follow an emotional path to accept the recommendation.

In McKinsey's USPS presentation, there are two sets of recommendations – one including standard actions and one including fundamental change actions. Of the two, the more powerful is the set of fundamental change actions. The two sets are an "and" not an "or," in the sense that both can be implemented to help improve USPS profitability. Additionally, one set need not be completed before the next one, so sequential order is not required. However, fundamental change is a hard pill to swallow.

A key principle in storytelling is that characters always take the minimum conservative action given the circumstances in which they find themselves. A hero will take radical, life-threatening actions, but only if there are no viable alternatives. This principle determines ordering for the USPS resolution. Organizations (almost) always start fixing problems by taking standard actions. They pursue fundamental change (only) when the standard actions fail to achieve the necessary results. So, due to risk aversion, McKinsey started with actions within USPS control, standard actions, as shown in slide #22 (Figure 5-3).

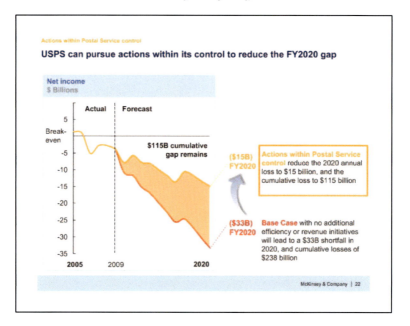

Figure 5-3: McKinsey's USPS presentation slide #22

The remainder of the resolution section is structured using most if not all of the key principles used to structure the situation section including bottom-line-up-front messaging, story-centric progression, and depth-order tree-traversal. Since there is considerable content here, I have broken the flow up into two pieces. The hierarchy exploring standard change actions is provided in Figure 5-4.

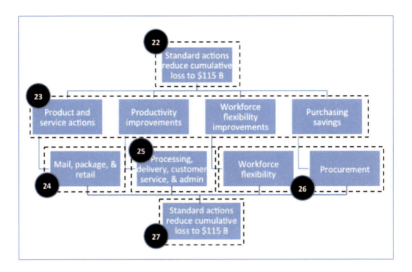

Figure 5-4: Structure for the "standard actions" part of the USPS resolution section

Slide #22 (Figure 5-3) provides the bottom-line-up-front impact of reducing cumulative losses from $238 billion to $115 billion through standard actions within USPS control. That information triggers the question "What standard actions achieve this and how much does each contribute to reducing the loss?" Slide #23 (Figure 5-5) provides the answer with four groups of standard actions plus avoided interest due to reduced debt. I would have started with productivity improvements as they offer the largest impact and sequential- and emotional- order are required here.

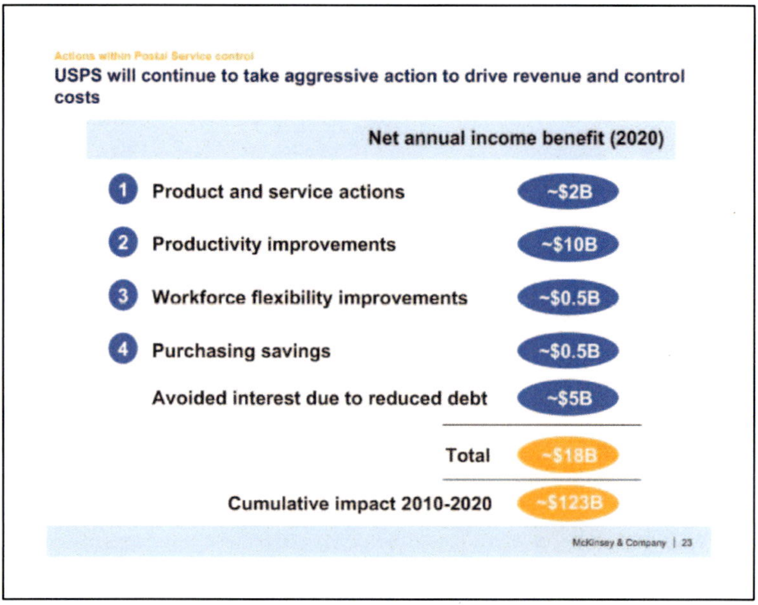

```
Actions within Postal Service control
USPS will continue to take aggressive action to drive revenue and control
costs

                                    Net annual income benefit (2020)

    ① Product and service actions              ~$2B

    ② Productivity improvements                ~$10B

    ③ Workforce flexibility improvements       ~$0.5B

    ④ Purchasing savings                       ~$0.5B

        Avoided interest due to reduced debt   ~$5B

                                    Total      ~$18B

                    Cumulative impact 2010-2020 ~$123B

                                              McKinsey & Company | 23
```

Figure 5-5: McKinsey's USPS presentation slide #23

Slide #24 (Figure 5-6), slide #25 (Figure 5-7), and slide #26 (Figure 5-8), detail the key actions to achieve, respectively: product and service initiatives; productivity improvements; and, workforce flexibility and procurement optimization.

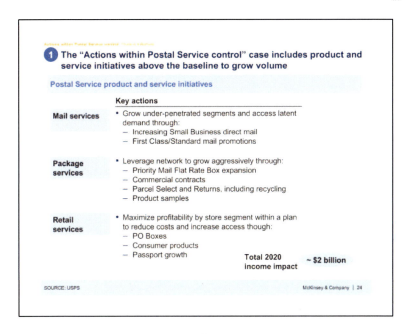

Figure 5-6: McKinsey's USPS presentation slide #24

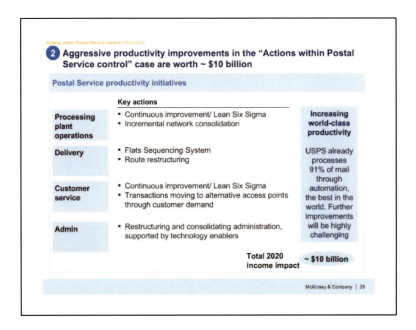

Figure 5-7: McKinsey's USPS presentation slide #25

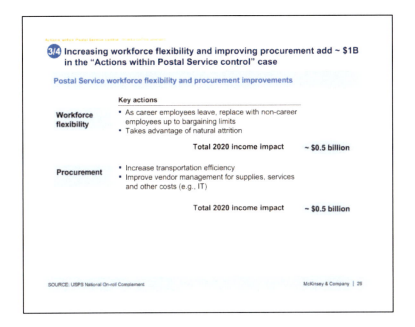

Figure 5-8: McKinsey's USPS presentation slide #26

Though not strictly necessary, the standard actions within USPS control part of the resolution section ends by repeating the bottom-line improvement in cumulative loss through 2020. This recapitulation in slide #27 (Figure 5-9), a technique common in dramatic storytelling, helps bring the audience out of the weeds and back to the main story progression. Actions within USPS control reduce the cumulative loss from $238 billion to $115 billion. Now, the audience is emotionally ready to ask the next question, "Are there more radical actions the USPS can take to change losses to profits?"

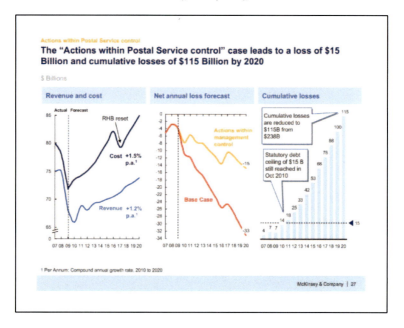

Figure 5-9: McKinsey's USPS presentation slide #27

Paralleling the first part of the resolution section, the second part begins with the full impact of fundamental change actions as shown in slide #28 (Figure 5-10). As illustrated, the additional actions, together with actions within USPS control, should yield positive net income well ahead of 2020.

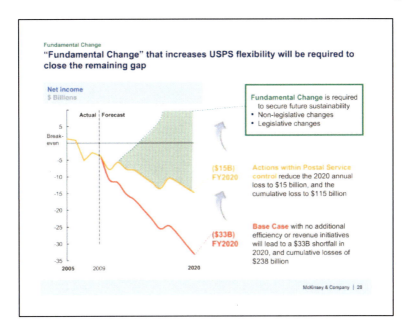

Figure 5-10: McKinsey's USPS presentation slide #28

The remainder of the fundamental change part of the resolution section is outlined in Figure 5-11. Once again, the now familiar content organization best practices apply, including: bottom-line-up-front messaging, story-centric progression, and depth-order tree-traversal.

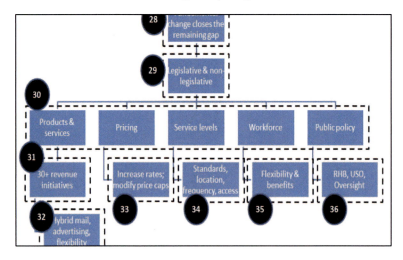

Figure 5-11: Structure for the "fundamental change" part of the USPS resolution section

Tip 28: Handle objections as they arise

As stated previously, characters in stories always take the minimum action required to address issues. In McKinsey's USPS presentation, the audience is primed to embrace fundamental change. But, even in dire circumstances, people may object to solutions that are too extreme. To stave off a major objection, the McKinsey team steps momentarily out of the narrative in slide #29 (Figure 5-12) to acknowledge certain changes will require legislative action. Because such actions are far more complex, legislative changes consistently appear *after* non-legislative changes on each of the coming slides.

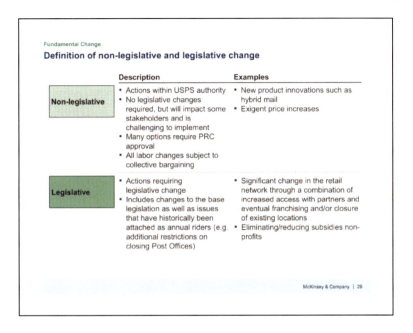

Figure 5-12: McKinsey's USPS presentation slide #29

Slide #30 (Figure 5-13) is the summary node for the remainder of the resolution section. It frames actions in two dimensions, first by the categories already familiar to the audience (products and services; pricing; etc.) and then by the new, more emotionally intense division of non-legislative versus legislative.

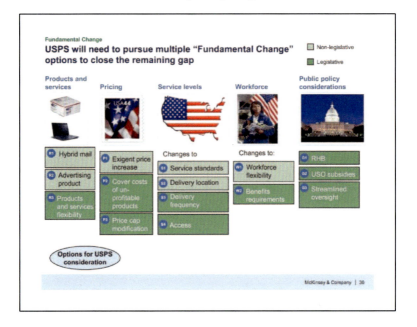

Figure 5-13: McKinsey's USPS presentation slide #30

The USPS's portfolio of products and services can be transformed in many ways. Recall that McKinsey was not the only consulting firm hired for this engagement. BCG provided the mail volume forecasts McKinsey used to model the base case. In addition, Accenture explored successful ways foreign posts have expanded their offerings – several of which are integrated in slide #31 (Figure 5-14). The presentation goes into further detail on the most attractive subset of action in slide #32 (Figure 5-15).

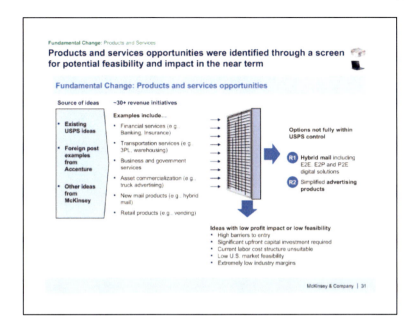

Figure 5-14: McKinsey's USPS presentation slide #31

Figure 5-15: McKinsey's USPS presentation slide #32

Slide #33 (Figure 5-16), slide #34 (Figure 5-17), slide #35 (Figure 5-18), and slide #36 (Figure 5-19), complete the detailed fundamental change recommendations for, respectively: pricing; service level; workforce; and, public policy.

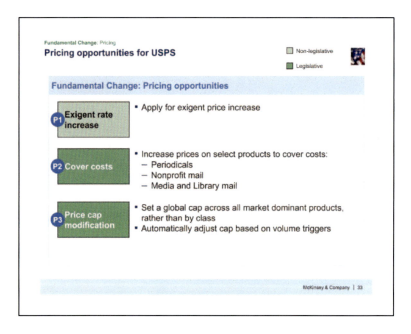

Figure 5-16: McKinsey's USPS presentation slide #33

Figure 5-17: McKinsey's USPS presentation slide #34

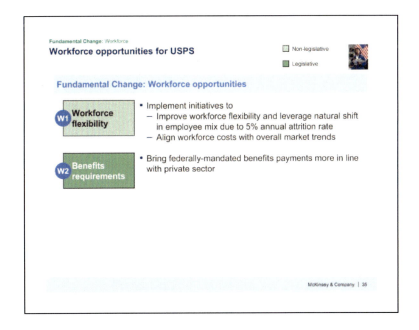

Figure 5-18: McKinsey's USPS presentation slide #35

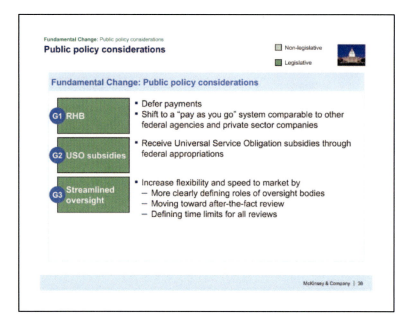

Figure 5-19: McKinsey's USPS presentation slide #36

Tip 29: Create an epilogue for critical information beyond the main storyline

Epilogues in dramatic storytelling appear after the main plot has ended and serve to reveal the fates of characters, wrap up loose ends, or hint at a sequel. (Note: An epilogue is different than an Appendix in that the former is presented while the latter serves only as reference material.) While common in movies, they are rare in presentations because the content in an epilogue can easily diminish the power of the recommendations just delivered.

After the transition in slide #37 (Figure 5-20), McKinsey delivers an epilogue in slide #38 (Figure 5-21). Recall, the primary storyline in the presentation concerns intermediate and long-term actions needed to return the USPS to profitability by 2020. By that measure, discussion of short-term concerns is out of context. However, this particular example illustrates that an epilogue is acceptable when the information is critical. While there is still a risk of diluting the recommendations in the main story, the McKinsey team must have felt a duty to inform the USPS decision makers of an imminent threat and to recommend further options to remain solvent. Even in the last slide, McKinsey held true to the practice of never showing a problem without suggesting a viable solution.

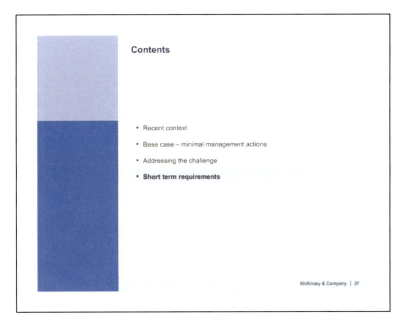

Figure 5-20: McKinsey's USPS presentation slide #37

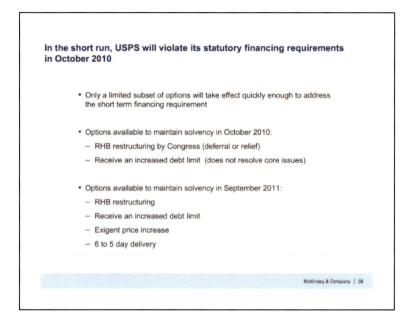

Figure 5-21: McKinsey's USPS presentation slide #38

* * * * *

For senior decision makers and general audiences, the level of detail in McKinsey's USPS resolution is sufficient. For instance, the recommendations frame what must be done as "change delivery location to curbside or cluster mailboxes." However, there is insufficient detail to fully realize the benefits of the recommendations.

I suspect that McKinsey also delivered a private project plan to the USPS, including the following:

- Owners of actions as well as key stakeholders
- Mindset strategy required for changes to stick in the organization's specific environment

- Leading and lagging key performance indicators (KPIs) to validate critical assumptions and measure the impact of actions to the business
- Timing of key milestones and critical activities
- Required resources and dependencies given the USPS's current and needed capabilities
- Potential people and process risks to be actively managed along with pre-mediated contingency plans
- Potential additional benefits which may be realized

Chapter 6

The Approach-Findings-Implications Framework

Tip 30: Use the Approach-Findings-Implications framework for informative presentations

The previous chapters explored the powerful situation-complication-resolution (SCR) framework approach to persuasive business storytelling. At its core, SCR is a general three-act story structure establishing background in Act I, challenges and opportunities in Act II, and proposed solutions in Act III. Stanford University communications professor Matt Abrahams generalizes the model even further as "What? So what? Now what?" At the end of the day, any set of synonyms will do as long as the problem-solution narrative remains.

By design, BCG's presentation to the USPS is light on persuasion and heavy on information. The firm's task was to build a model to predict the "base case" for Standard Mail volume through 2020. Since its presentation describes the model and its result, BCG transformed SCR into approach-findings-implications. Different words, same story.

Tip 31: Avoid presenting the random walk you followed in your research process

Occasionally, novice presenters build approach-findings-implications presentations that meander linearly through their research process. Unless the *entire* point of your presentation is to detail the discovery process, as in hunting for a cure for a debilitating disease, avoid sharing false starts, wrong turns, and random bits of information. Give your audience only what it needs, no less and no more, to comprehend your story, decide, and take action. Stanford University professor Matt Abrahams teaches his students this tip using the following metaphor: Tell the time, don't build the clock. BCG, no novice at presenting insights, did not fall into this trap.

(Note: Many scientific presentations require a rigorous overview of the methodology researchers used to conduct an experiment. Moreover, there is often as much value in revealing tests that did not work as there is in sharing tests that did. The overarching rule then, for academia and business, is to give the audience what it wants in the order it expects.)

Chapter 7

BCG's USPS Approach

McKinsey's overarching strategy presentation relied on two inputs from other management consulting organizations. Accenture studied lucrative, non-mail products offered by postal services outside the United States. The Boston Consulting Group (BCG), the focus of this chapter, projected US mail volumes to 2020, assuming a business-as-usual scenario.

The title slide (Figure 7-1) makes it crystal clear that audience members should expect to see a robust, ten-year projection of US mail volumes (and hopefully not much more).

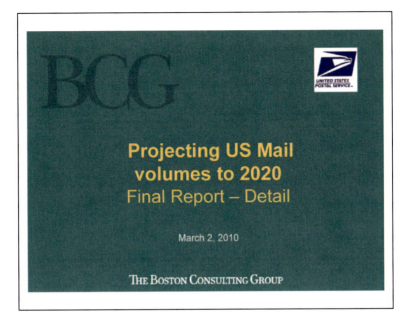

Figure 7-1: BCG's USPS presentation slide #0

Curiously, and counter to the best-practice applied by McKinsey, BCG dives directly into Act I of its strategic story without using an agenda slide to serve as a roadmap. While the section introduction divider slide (Figure 7-2) signals a transition, the audience would benefit from knowing how the story will unfold. The overall architecture of the presentation is as follows:[8]

- Act I: Objectives and approach
- Act II: Results (and benchmarks from other global posts)
- Act III: Implications

---

[8] BCG's presentation also has an extensive Appendix not included here

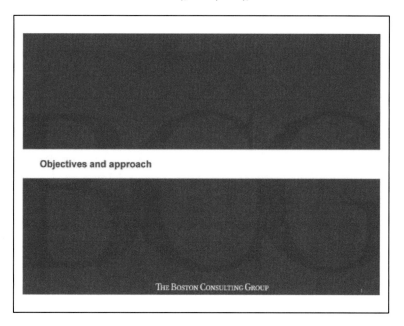

Figure 7-2: BCG's USPS presentation slide #1

Slide #2 (Figure 7-3) outlines the overall objective of projecting base case mail volumes to 2020. Since "base case" may be unfamiliar, the phrase is immediately explained as the "business-as-usual scenario." This slide continues to answer questions as they arise by covering, "OK then, what are you assuming to be business-as-usual?"

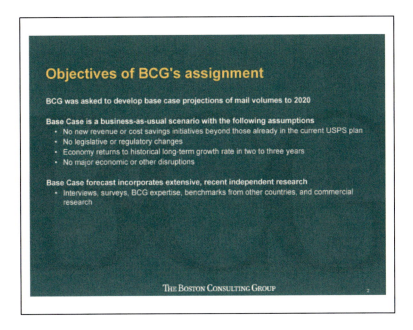

Figure 7-3: BCG's USPS presentation slide #2

The natural next question is, "What approach did you use to build the forecast?" I feel it is redundant to have previewed this on slide #2 (Figure 7-3) in the block of text entitled, "Base case forecast incorporates extensive, recent independent research" since the answer is covered in complete detail on slide #3 (Figure 7-4). The approach BCG used is typical of best-practice strategy consulting engagements and includes quantitative and qualitative insights gleaned from internal and external sources.

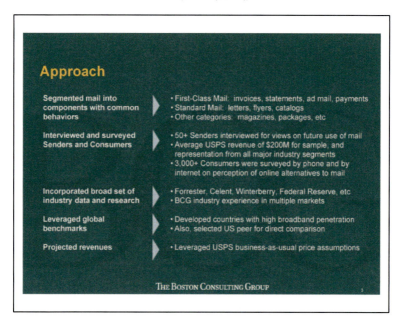

Figure 7-4: BCG's USPS presentation slide #3

Slide #3 (Figure 7-4) looks a lot like a summary node slide. As such, a reasonable audience member would expect the presentation to progress in one of two ways. First, if the approach were covered in adequate detail, then the presentation can move directly to the results section (Act II). Second, if the approach has further subtlety, then the presentation should progress through the additional complexity in the *approach* to segmentation, interviews, industry insights, global benchmarks, and projected revenues. In this type of presentation, I stress "double-clicking" on the *approach* only; any actual findings belong in the next section.

At first, BCG appears to have chosen to explore the subtleties of its approach. Slide #4 (Figure 7-5) delves into the first item in the progression with an overview of segmentation into First-Class and Standard Mail categories.

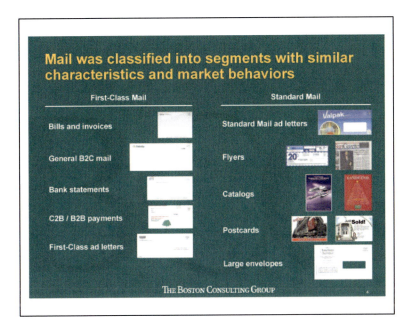

Figure 7-5: BCG's USPS presentation slide #4

By revealing the actual quantitative segmentation, slide #5 (Figure 7-6) violates the rule to only explore details of the approach. Moreover, the "Objectives and approach" section, and thus Act I, ends abruptly without similar treatment of the other key findings areas, including: interviews, industry insights, global benchmarks, and projected revenues.

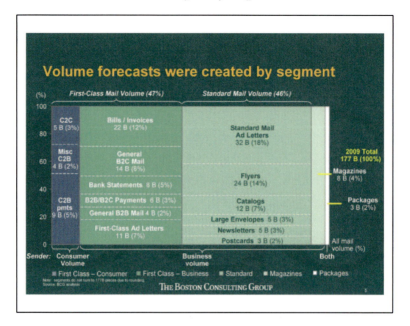

Figure 7-6: BCG's USPS presentation slide #5

* * * * *

Although deeper details in BCG's story feel somewhat incomplete, the audience does have a high-level sense of the approach the firm used to develop a forecast for USPS mail volume though 2020. Now, we are ready to discover what they found.

Chapter 8

BCG's USPS Findings

BCG's strategic story moves into Act II with the "Results" section divider shown in slide #6 (Figure 8-1). Here, following the bottom-line-up-front best practice, I would have expected the section to start with total forecasted volume through 2020. However, the section actually starts with what appears to be another slide further detailing the approach to segmentation details in slide #7 (Figure 8-2).

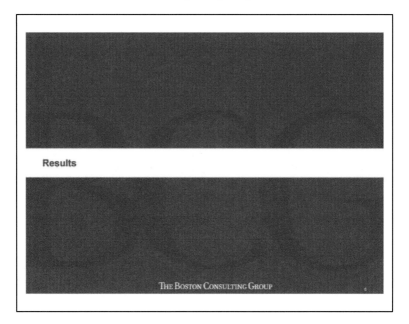

Figure 8-1: BCG's USPS presentation slide #6

Previously, BCG segmented mail into two categories, First-Class and Standard; in slide #7 (Figure 8-2), packages are introduced as an unexpected third category. Packages come and go randomly throughout the remainder of the presentation. In dramatic storytelling, the analogy is of an important character dropping in and out of the story with no rhyme or reason.

The slide goes on to mix apples (types of mail) with oranges (other metrics), compounding the confusion. To make matters even worse, the "Forecast" details on slide #7 (Figure 8-2) cover near term projections for the remainder of 2009 rather than what the audience is expecting, the forecast for 2020 as the slide title implies.

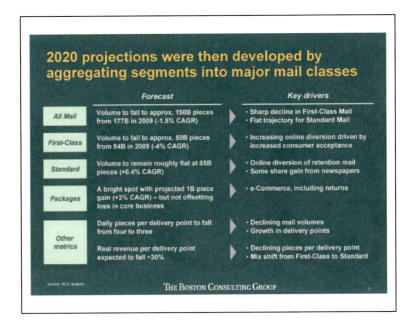

Figure 8-2: BCG's USPS presentation slide #7

Slide #8 (Figure 8-3) gives the audience exactly what it was expecting had the previous slide not derailed the story. Since the slide title discusses a drop of 15%, we must presume the sender perspective, rather than the consumer perspective or the worst-case benchmark, represents the "base case" volume forecast.

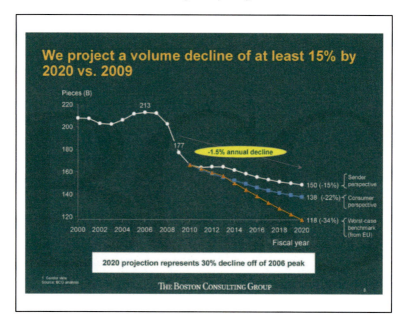

Figure 8-3: BCG's USPS presentation slide #8

To properly carry the story forward, BCG must answer the most pressing question triggered by slide #8 (Figure 8-3), "Why is the volume projected to decline by at least 15% by 2020?" To answer this question the designer must choose between the Standard/First-Class Mail segmentation and the sender/consumer/worst-case scenario segmentation as dominant. BCG chose the mail segmentation. Given that mail categories were introduced as "characters" in Act I, this was the correct path as shown in slide #9 (Figure 8-4).

Figure 8-4: BCG's USPS presentation slide #9

Even without being able to assess the impact of each of the trends in slide #9 (Figure 8-4), one gets the sense that the reason for the volume decline is a confluence of negative trends for USPS; in total, there are nine red down arrows compared to five green up arrows. The story continues in an effective manner by showing the result of these qualitative forces on the quantitative volumes for First-Class Mail and Standard Mail in slide #10 (Figure 8-5) and slide #11 (Figure 8-6), respectively.

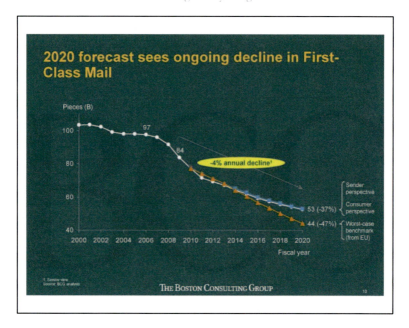

Figure 8-5: BCG's USPS presentation slide #10

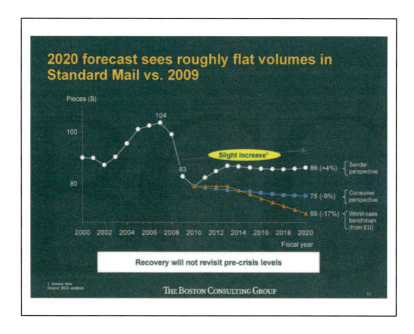

Figure 8-6: BCG's USPS presentation slide #11

Following the preceding pair of slides, BCG logically continues the results section as shown in slide #12 (Figure 8-7) with a complete detail of the mix of mail types within the First-Class and Standard Mail segments.

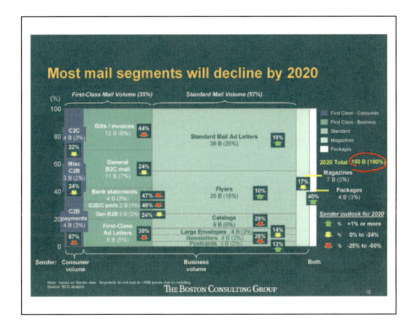

Figure 8-7: BCG's USPS presentation slide #12

Then BCG shifts, for reasons that defy explanation from a narrative flow point of view, from the Standard Mail/First-Class Mail segmentation to the sender/customer/worst-case perspective segmentation in slide #13 (Figure 8-8). While the sender perspective is most likely the "base case" forecast, the results section needs the missing customer and worst-case perspectives to be complete.

Figure 8-8: BCG's USPS presentation slide #13

Introduced by the divider in slide #14 (Figure 8-9), the information in the "Benchmarks from other global posts" section is just another set of findings; therefore this next section is still part of Act II.

Figure 8-9: BCG's USPS presentation slide #14

Though not immediately clear how the foreign post volume trends in slide #15 (Figure 8-10) factor into BCG's mail volume model for USPS, the root-cause insight of broadband penetration illustrated in slide #16 (Figure 8-11) is fascinating. The essence of this finding was already expressed in slide #9 (Figure 8-4), which showed the positive and negative trends affecting USPS volume. Consequently, the entire "Benchmarks from other global posts" section belongs in the Appendix.

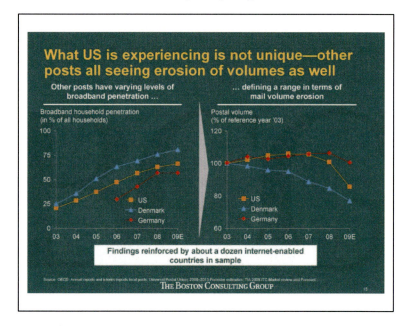

Figure 8-10: BCG's USPS presentation slide #15

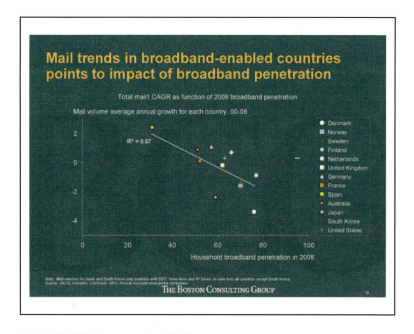

Figure 8-11: BCG's USPS presentation slide #16

* * * * *

Getting reoriented, Act I of BCG's strategy story described their *approach* for projecting USPS mail volume through 2020. The just completed Act II shared the *findings* gleaned using this approach. Next, BCG's story moves on to explore the *implications* of those findings.

Chapter 9

BCG's USPS Implications

BCG's presentation transitions to Act III at the divider in slide #17 (Figure 9-1). Given the section title "Implications" – presumably of the projected 15% decline in mail volume through 2020, two questions arise: The first, "How should the USPS respond (i.e., downsize) to the volume decrease?" The second, "What, if anything, can be done to turn the negative volume trend around?"

Figure 9-1: BCG's USPS presentation slide #17

I would never expect a discussion of revenue per delivery point as shown in slide #18 (Figure 9-2) to begin this section since it is such a leap from the core theme of volume and requires pricing assumptions not previously addressed. Again, using a story analogy, this is akin to introducing a major character in the final act with zero foreshadowing – a serious "no-no" in storytelling.

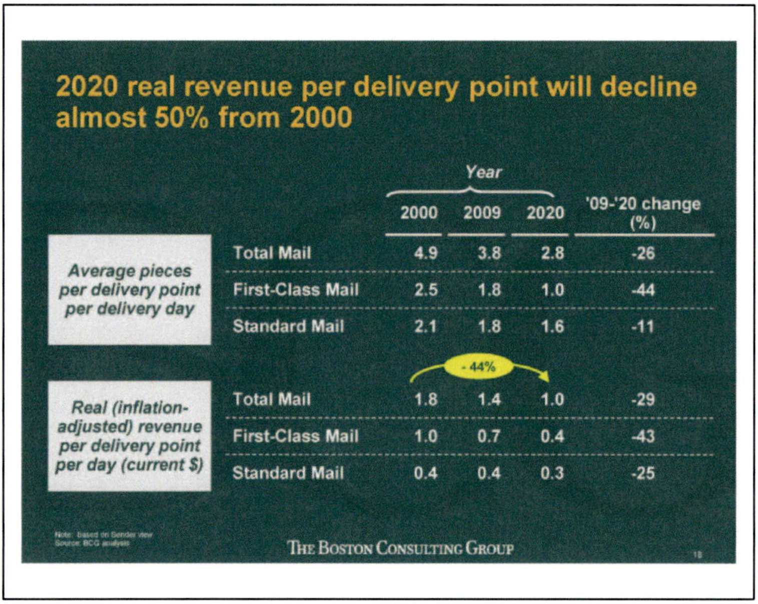

2020 real revenue per delivery point will decline almost 50% from 2000

		Year			'09-'20 change (%)
		2000	2009	2020	
Average pieces per delivery point per delivery day	Total Mail	4.9	3.8	2.8	-26
	First-Class Mail	2.5	1.8	1.0	-44
	Standard Mail	2.1	1.8	1.6	-11
Real (inflation-adjusted) revenue per delivery point per day (current $)	Total Mail	1.8	1.4	1.0	-29
	First-Class Mail	1.0	0.7	0.4	-43
	Standard Mail	0.4	0.4	0.3	-25

Note: based on Sender view
Source: BCG analysis

THE BOSTON CONSULTING GROUP

Figure 9-2: BCG's USPS presentation slide #18

The BCG team must have sensed that the shift to revenue was out of context since their presentation shifts back to volume in slide #19 (Figure 9-3). Of all the slides in the presentation, this one bothers me the most. Now, I appreciate a good sensitivity analysis as much as anyone, however, BCG already covered three scenarios in the form of the sender/customer/worst-case perspectives. Then to insert a light-weight +/- 10% sensitivity analysis here significantly diminishes the credibility of the work that went into developing the model.

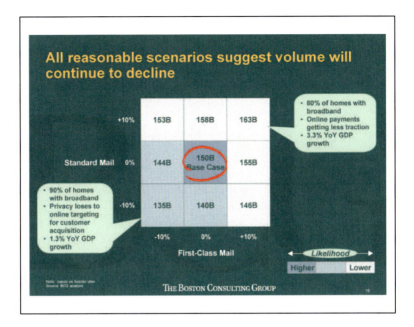

Figure 9-3: BCG's USPS presentation slide #19

Slide #20 (Figure 9-4) further erodes the credibility of the presentation and the model by preemptively explaining why the BCG forecast may end up being wrong. (For the record, McKinsey did this, too.) These overwhelmingly negative factors should have been inputs into the scenarios instead, especially the worst-case scenario. However, I do not believe this degree of rigor was applied given the location of this slide in the presentation.

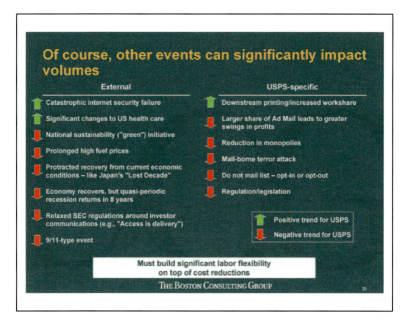

Figure 9-4: BCG's USPS presentation slide #20

The statement in the white box at the bottom of slide #20 (Figure 9-4) triggers the question, "How can we build significant labor flexibility?" This question is answered with structural changes enumerated on slide #21 (Figure 9-5), including examples adopted by posts outside of the United States as detailed in slide #22 (Figure 9-6).

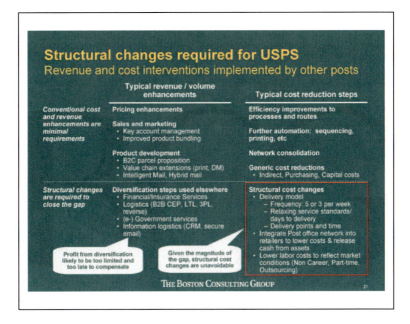

Figure 9-5: BCG's USPS presentation slide #21

Figure 9-6: BCG's USPS presentation slide #22

Slide #23 (Figure 9-7) would have been better placed at the beginning of the "Implications" section where Act III could have effectively explored the recommended changes to the USPS's delivery model, branch network, and labor model in response to the expected volume decline. Instead by being placed at the end of the presentation, the slide ends up triggering questions. Dramatic stories *only* do that when the producers have committed to releasing a sequel. In general, business presentations should be completely self-contained with *all questions resolved* by the final slide.

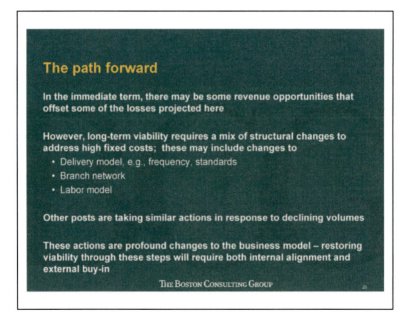

Figure 9-7: BCG's USPS presentation slide #23

* * * * *

I have hammered away pretty hard on the BCG presentation because it contains errors that significantly disrupt the flow of the story. Since I do not like to criticize without proposing improvements, I now offer the narrative progression I would have used:

- Act 1 (Situation - Objective and Approach):
    - Our objective is to forecast USPS "base case" mail volume through 2020, inclusive of Standard Mail and First-Class Mail segments.
    - Our partner on this engagement, McKinsey, will integrate this volume projection with separately developed pricing and cost projections, to build an overall view of USPS profitability.
    - Our approach consisted of building the overall forecast in bottom-up fashion from forecasts for every mail sub-segment within the two major segments
    - The sub-segment forecasts are based on quantitative information (e.g., time-series data models, foreign post data, etc.) and qualitative information (e.g., positive and negative macro trends, consumer and sender surveys, etc.).
- Act II (Complication – Findings):

- Our "base case" forecast calls for a 15% decline in total mail volume through 2020.
- The "base case" breaks down into the two segments as follows... and further into the sub-segments as follows...
- The "base case" forecast relies on the following critical assumptions referenced in our approach... Violation of the assumptions leads to the following best-case (x% likelihood) and worst-case (y% likelihood) scenarios...

- Act III (Resolution – Implications):
  - Given the expected 15% "base case" volume decline, we recommend the USPS make the following structural changes to its delivery model, branch network, and labor model.
  - The following key performance indicators KPIs) signal evolution toward the best-case scenario. In that event, the USPS should take the following actions to take advantage of the positive momentum.
  - The following key performance indicators KPIs) signal evolution toward the worst-case scenario. In that event, the USPS should take the following actions to mitigate the impact of the negative momentum.

Having seen best-practice storytelling in McKinsey's USPS presentation and significant issues in the narrative structure of BCG's, we can now apply what we have learned so far to Accenture's presentation.

Chapter 10

The Situation-Opportunity-Resolution Framework

Each of the three strategy consulting organizations presented its findings to help the United States Postal Service find a path toward profitability using a different framework.

- McKinsey used the ubiquitous situation-complication-resolution framework. This should be your go-to framework most of the time when you want to persuade business audiences.

- BCG used the approach-results-implications framework, a worthy alternative when your material is more focused on sharing information than on securing a decision.

- Accenture, the focus of the next several chapters, used situation-opportunity-resolution (SOR), a subtle variation on SCR that comes in handy when you want decision makers to act in order to capture a set of benefits.

The storytelling function of the situation in SOR is identical to that of the situation in SCR – to establish the historical context that led to the current state, whether good, neutral, or bad.

In the SCR framework, the complication creates negative tension either by threatening a current positive state or by exacerbating a current negative state. In McKinsey's SCR-based story, the complication is a set of forces or trends expected to turn a significant loss into a catastrophic loss. In the SOR framework, the opportunity creates positive tension either by offering to propel a positive current state to higher heights or by reversing a negative current state. You can create just as much story tension by dangling a reward for a protagonist to win as you can by creating an obstacle for a protagonist to avoid.

In both the SCR and SOR frameworks the resolution releases the tension. The former does so by prescribing a solution to the complication and the latter by showing how to capture the opportunity.

While not always the case, the emotional tone in SCR shifts from positive to negative to positive as the three acts of the story unfold. Comparatively, the emotional tone in SOR usually moves from negative to positive to more positive. As such, SCR tends to be more emotionally intense and is therefore the better choice when your audience does not know it has a problem. SOR, in contrast, starts by acknowledging a problem with which the audience is often already familiar and quickly lets in the sunshine. Since the USPS hired not one but three consulting firms to find a path to profitability, the SOR framework used by Accenture is an excellent contrasting narrative choice.

Before I dive into Accenture's presentation, I need to stress one last time that SOR is a subtle variant of SCR. People familiar with SCR often treat the complication as something that disrupts the situation either positively or negatively. I do this myself and encourage you to do the same.

Chapter 11

Accenture's USPS Situation

Accenture's title in slide #0 (Figure 11-1) nicely frames the pursuit of an opportunity: "Is Diversification the Answer to Mail Woes? The Experience of International Posts."

Figure 11-1: Accenture's USPS presentation slide #0

Tip 32: Protect your intellectual property and limit your legal liability

Almost by definition, persuasive business presentations contain material, non-public information valuable to any third-party looking to gain an edge, including investors, competitors, suppliers, and even customers. For this reason, it is a good idea to include a notice of confidentiality and non-disclosure as Accenture did in slide #1 (Figure 11-2). Of course, as with all legal matters, consult an attorney for language and required practices to adequately protect your intellectual property. For instance, some jurisdictions may require specific language in the footer of every slide.

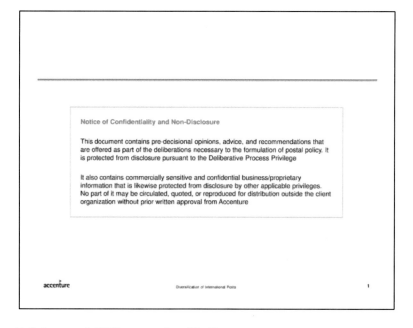

Figure 11-2: Accenture's USPS presentation slide #1

If your jurisdiction does not provide protection or if you waive your protection implicitly or explicitly, there is no need to delay the start of your story with legalese. The "deliberative process privilege" referred to by Accenture is a common-law principle that protects information concerning internal processes from public disclosure even though taxpayer money funded the work. However, I am able to reproduce their presentation here because I obtained permission from the consulting firm and from the United States Postal Service. In addition, because my intent is republication for critical and educational purposes, I am protected under the Fair Use provision of United States copyright law.

I mention this because you need to be very careful about reproducing material you find. Attribution, though always required, may be insufficient. When in doubt, ask an attorney or find an unambiguously legal alternative.

Titled "About this document," slide #2 (Figure 11-3) protects Accenture from legal liability by framing the presentation as information rather than advice. To that end, the title of "Disclaimer" would be more accurate. I find this sort of hedge disingenuous (like fortune tellers claiming their services are "for entertainment purposes only" or skydiving outfits requiring liability waivers). But if this tactic provides legal protection in certain jurisdictions, far be it from me to recommend otherwise. Such language is typically not required for presentations developed and delivered internally.

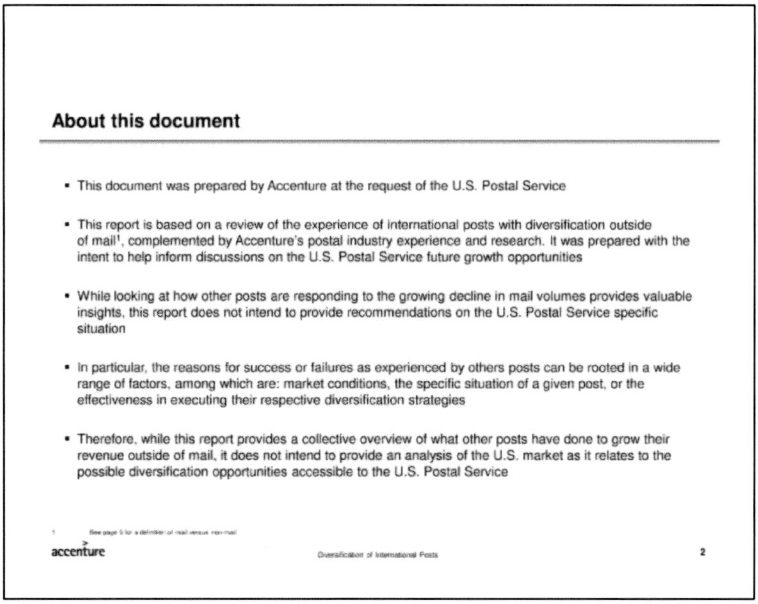
About this document
This document was prepared by Accenture at the request of the U.S. Postal Service
This report is based on a review of the experience of international posts with diversification outside of mail[1], complemented by Accenture's postal industry experience and research. It was prepared with the intent to help inform discussions on the U.S. Postal Service future growth opportunities
While looking at how other posts are responding to the growing decline in mail volumes provides valuable insights, this report does not intend to provide recommendations on the U.S. Postal Service specific situation
In particular, the reasons for success or failures as experienced by others posts can be rooted in a wide range of factors, among which are: market conditions, the specific situation of a given post, or the effectiveness in executing their respective diversification strategies
Therefore, while this report provides a collective overview of what other posts have done to grow their revenue outside of mail, it does not intend to provide an analysis of the U.S. market as it relates to the possible diversification opportunities accessible to the U.S. Postal Service
accenture
Diversification of International Posts
2

Figure 11-3: Accenture's USPS presentation slide #2

Tip 33: Do not include an "Executive Summary" at the beginning of your presentation

Books, plays, and movies take you on dramatic journeys. By the same token, the most compelling business presentations are a form of strategic storytelling leading listeners down a controlled path. To illustrate this, you find ample foreshadowing but no executive summary at the beginning of Shakespeare's Hamlet. It would be much harder to sit through the play if Horatio, one of the survivors of the ensuing massacre, recounted the tale of the Danish prince's demise to Fortinbras, the invading Prince of Norway, at the beginning of the play instead of at the end.

A business presentation simply begins with a compelling, SMART title to tell the audience where you are going. Executive summaries are often dense, bulleted lists of text spanning one or two slides. If you have ever delivered one, you know how tedious they are to get through. Worse, they raise more questions than can be answered in detail. Finally, once you deliver an executive summary you might as well end the meeting since there is little more to share.

That said, I can think of only two times when an executive summary is appropriate:

- First, at the beginning of a presentation designed for reading, not for delivery. By being included in a document, the executive summary serves its purpose of giving readers all the essential findings without having to spend time on details.

- Second, as the last slide in a presentation. In that position, it serves as a recap which the presenter may verbally deliver or, as is more often the case, simply let exist on screen while answering questions and wrapping up the discussion. Putting the executive summary in the Appendix is another variation of this exception to the rule.

The McKinsey USPS presentation did not contain an executive summary, similarly, the BCG USPS presentation did not give away the bacon either. Conversely, as shown in slide #3 (Figure 11-4), the Accenture USPS presentation *does* have an executive summary.

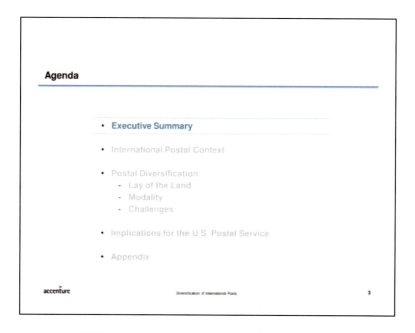

Figure x: Accenture's USPS presentation slide #3

Accenture's executive summary consists of two-parts. The first part is actually not an executive summary at all but a set of three slides detailing the firm's objective and approach as shown in slide #4 (Figure 11-5), slide #5 (Figure 11-6), and slide #6 (Figure 11-7). Although an objective can be embedded in the presentation title and accompanying talk track, restatement is useful on a dedicated slide when the material is to be shared as a report and when the scope of the work requires explanation – both of which hold in this case. Similarly, the approach should reside in the Appendix unless the target audience needs it to have sufficient context for the story and confidence in the presenter. Accenture's approach provides for both needs because it conveys comprehensiveness in methodology and thoroughness of coverage.

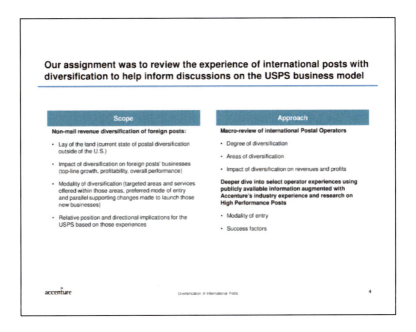

Figure 11-5: Accenture's USPS presentation slide #4

124 Strategic Storytelling

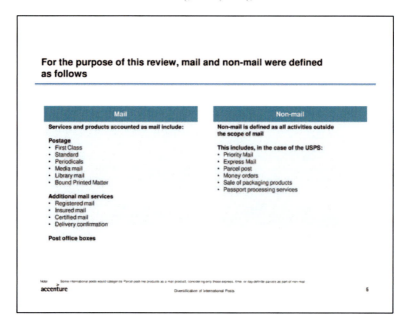

Figure 11-6: Accenture's USPS presentation slide #5

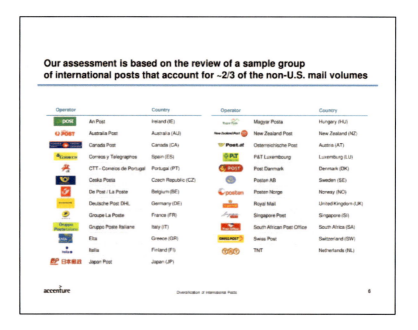

Figure 11-7: Accenture's USPS presentation slide #6

Slide #7 (Figure 11-8) and slide #8 (Figure 11-9) provide a dense and traditional executive summary. In reading the slides closely you get the full situation-opportunity-resolution narrative in compact form. If you are going to do an executive summary, this is the way to do it. I would have moved these two slides to the end of the presentation (or to the Appendix) and renamed the section "Approach and Objectives." Furthermore, I imagine that Accenture did not include the two "Key Conclusions" slides (or at least did not speak to them) when they delivered the presentation since doing so would have taken too long and given away too much.

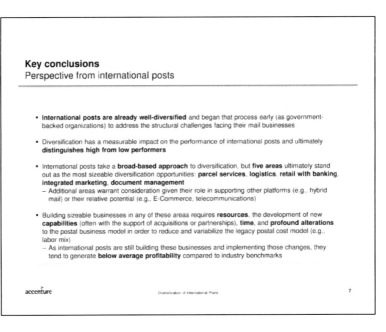

Figure 11-8: Accenture's USPS presentation slide #7

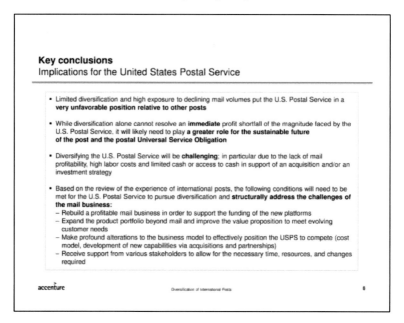

Figure 11-9: Accenture's USPS presentation slide #8

Like McKinsey, Accenture appears to favor the word "context" over "situation," as shown in slide #9 (Figure 11-10). Rather than using the lone word or the similarly vague "Recent Context," Accenture provides more clarity via specificity with "International Postal Context." Best practice would have required an action verb such as "Review" at the front of the bullet to put the audience in the right mental mode for the section.

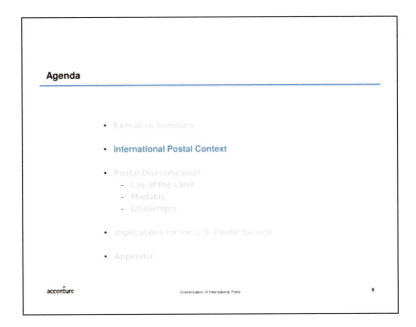

Figure 11-10: Accenture's USPS presentation slide #9

Figure 11-12 illustrates the complete organizing structure of Accenture's USPS situation.

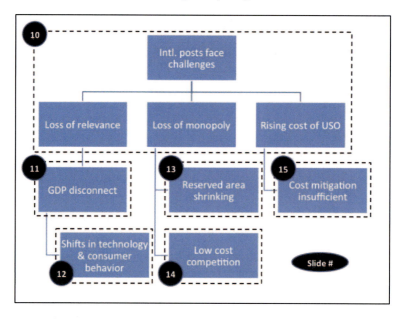

Figure 11-12: Outline of Accenture's USPS situation

Accenture's entire situation is expertly encapsulated in the title of slide #10 (Figure 11-13): "International posts are facing major challenges with their mail business." If the audience fully accepts this statement, the presenter could move directly to the opportunity section. More likely, listeners will want to know, "Which major challenges?" Since this summary node slide frames the remainder of the situation, it outlines the key challenges.

Figure 11-13: Accenture's USPS presentation slide #10

Tip 34: Annotations at the bottom of a slide should only be used to transition to the next slide

Sometimes the title and content on a slide trigger more than one natural question. In those circumstances, an annotation (also known as a call-out) at the bottom of the slide can make the transition to the next slide explicit. Thus, it can play a critical role in the flow of the story.

Unfortunately, the annotation at the bottom of slide #10 (Figure 11-13) – "They pursue diversification as a means to structurally address their challenges" – is doing the unexpected. The annotation rather abruptly links the challenges to the solution; or stated in the terminology of our framework, linking the situation to the resolution.

This not only jumps the gun by prematurely leapfrogging the opportunity section, it also breaks the narrative flow since the next set of slides has nothing to do with diversification or other structural changes. Moreover, there is no ambiguity in what should come next, a deeper discussion of the "loss of relevance" challenge. Consequently, this annotation should be removed.

Tip 35: Prove bold claims

After the summary node slide, Accenture's USPS presentation explores the first challenge facing international posts – loss of relevance. Since that is a bold claim, an audience will ask, "What proof do you have?" The proof is the analysis in slide #11 (Figure 11-14) showing letter volume has recently become disconnected from GDP growth.

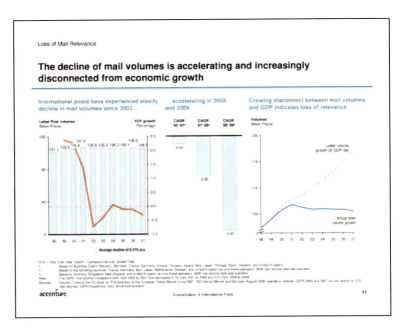

Figure 11-14: Accenture's USPS presentation slide #11

The audience now knows letter volume has become disconnected from GDP after many years of trending together but does not yet know why. Slide #12 (Figure 11-15) provides the answer. The historical drivers linked to GDP growth such as population expansion, increasing per-capita income, and increased mobility still exist; however, two forces are overwhelming those drivers. First, technological advances such as electronic payment and digitization of information are eliminating printed account statements and catalogues. Second, shifting consumer behavior related to environmental concerns, security, and convenience are compounding the problem for snail mail.

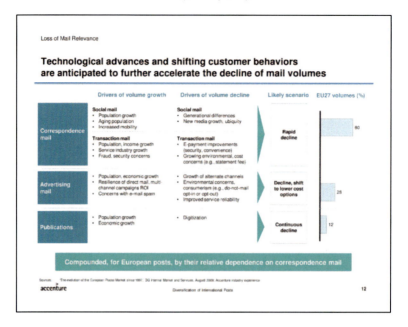

Figure 11-15: Accenture's USPS presentation slide #12

Tip 36: Use ellipses in slide titles to support the flow of the story

In slide #13 (Figure 11-16) and slide #14 (Figure 11-17), the situation transitions to the next challenge - loss of postal monopoly. The use of ellipses (…) at the end of one slide title and the beginning of the next is a technique usually reserved for instances where the second slide answers a question triggered by the first. In this instance, however, "… as" at the beginning of slide #14 simply indicates that an additional independent factor is at play. You can see this if you reverse the order of the titles as follows: "Lower cost competitors are gaining share from legacy postal operators in liberalized markets…"

"… as the elimination of the postal monopoly is likely to exacerbate the structural decline of mail volumes." Since the two factors could be reordered, I presume Accenture discusses the shrinking reserved area before low-cost competition because the former is the bigger issue.

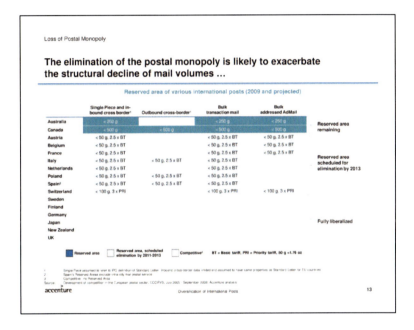

Figure 11-16: Accenture's USPS presentation slide #13

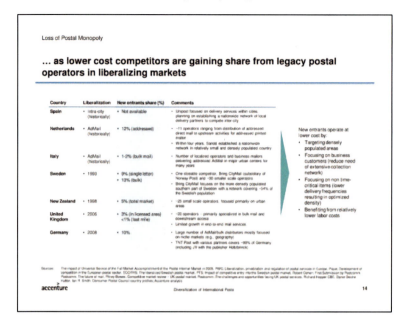

Figure 11-17: Accenture's USPS presentation slide #14

Slide #15 (Figure 11-18) outlines the profitability struggles with which international posts are dealing in the face of rising Universal Service Obligation (USO) costs. This slide is a nice story-within-a-story, showing mitigation tactics are not curbing costs quickly enough.

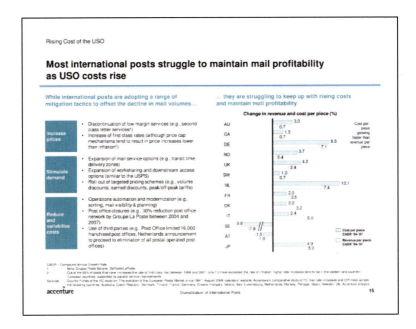

Figure 11-18: Accenture's USPS presentation (slide #15)

* * * * *

Postal services around the world are struggling with loss of relevance, loss of monopoly, and rising costs for their Universal Service Obligation (USO). The answer to "What should posts do to address these challenges?" is the focus of the next Act in Accenture's strategic story.

Chapter 12

Accenture's USPS Opportunity

Back on slide #10 (Figure 11-13), Accenture foreshadowed diversification into non-mail products and services as the opportunity postal services around the world must embrace to address their common set of challenges.

Though rigorously structured and easy to understand, Act II of Accenture's USPS diversification story is rather involved. As represented in slide #16 (Figure 12-1), Accenture's opportunity section, aptly named "Postal Diversification," contains three subsections. In story terms, think of these as three scenes we expect to be connected together progressively by tension tied to open questions. The first scene, "Lay of the land," introduces diversification as an effective means of addressing the challenges to profitability. The second section, "Modality," begins by sharing the mutually-exclusive and collectively-exhaustive set of diversification options available and ends by prioritizing the most attractive subset. (I am not a huge fan of the term "Modality" since few audience members will intuitively know what that means; "Review diversification options" would have been far clearer.) Finally, the third section, "Challenges," explores structural changes required to successfully diversify. (Accenture's choice for the sub-section title is also puzzling here; "Explore diversification requirements" would have been superior.)

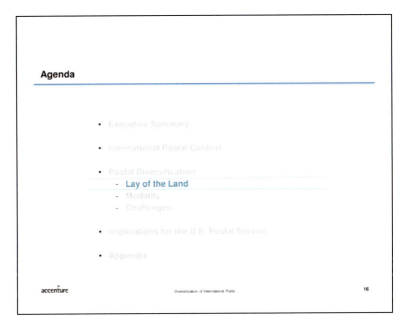

Figure 12-1: Accenture's USPS presentation slide #16

Figure 12-2 illustrates the structure for the "Lay of the land" subsection. Accenture used the set of techniques for strategic storytelling with which we are now thoroughly familiar, including: bottom-line-up-front messaging, summary nodes, depth order tree traversal, and the question-answer-narrative flow.

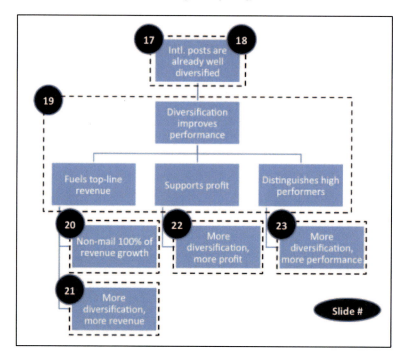

Figure 12-2: Structure of Accenture's USPS "Lay of the Land" subsection

Tip 37: Give each slide an independent title

Slide #17 (Figure 12-3) and slide #18 (Figure 12-4) provide the bottom-line-up-front message: international posts are already well diversified. The first of the two slides provides conclusive proof by showing not only that the majority of posts derive 40% or more of their revenue from non-mail, but also that non-mail represents the majority of revenue across the entire sample. The second of the two slides reveals which posts are included in their sample.

The one nit I have to pick with this pair of slides lies in repeating the title. I would keep the existing title for slide #17 (Figure 12-3), minus the "(I)." Slide #18 (Figure 12-4) could have many titles, but the "right"' title should answer a question raised by the previous slide and trigger a question to be answered by the next one. The column chart on the left-hand-side of the prior slide leaves the audience wanting to know, "Which international posts are in each diversification range?" The next slide, #19 (Figure 12-5), establishes the case that diversification correlates with profitability. Hence, slide #18 (Figure 12-4) should raise a question that prompts this case. I would go with the title, "Diversification is a Global Phenomenon." (Note: Using "The USPS Is Under-Diversified Relative to Global Benchmarks" is an excellent title, but not here since this part of the story is not about the USPS.)

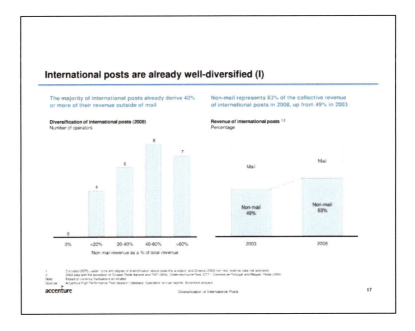

Figure 12-3: Accenture's USPS presentation slide #17

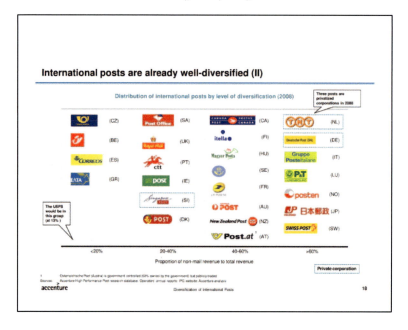

Figure 12-4: Accenture's USPS presentation slide #18

Just because international posts have diversified and are now deriving the majority of their revenue from non-mail products and services does not *necessarily* mean diversification is a good thing. To prove it is a boon, Accenture frames the three-part case in slide #19 (Figure 12-5).

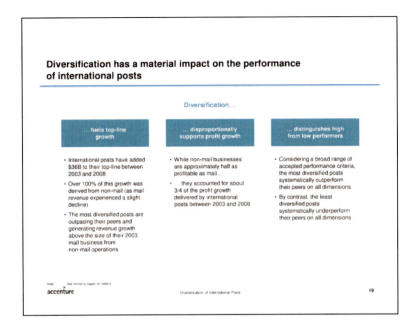

Figure 12-5: Accenture's USPS presentation slide #19

The remaining slides in the "Lay of the land" subsection, slides #20 to #23 (Figures 12-6 to 12-9), offer quantitative proof that higher levels of diversification lead to sustainable revenue and profit growth as well as efficient use of capital.

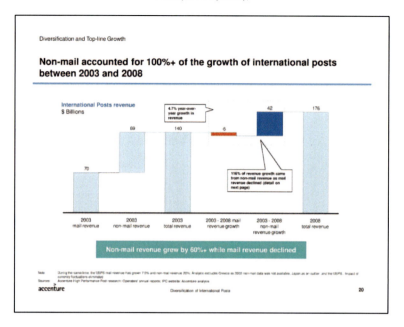

Figure 12-6: Accenture's USPS presentation slide #20

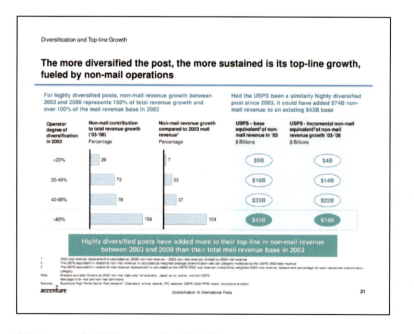

Figure 12-7: Accenture's USPS presentation slide #21

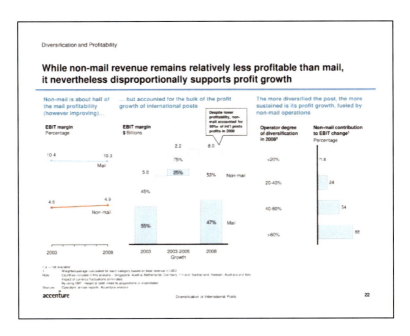

Figure 12-8: Accenture's USPS presentation slide #22

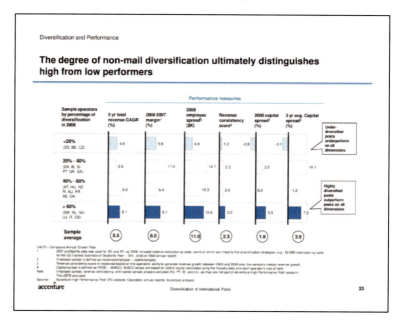

Figure 12-9: Accenture's USPS presentation slide #23

Accenture's USPS opportunity continues in the "Modality" subsection as shown in slide #24 (Figure 12-10). This title means the way in which something is done or, in this context, the non-mail products and services to which international posts have turned. Again, I wish the section had been more clearly titled, "Review diversification options."

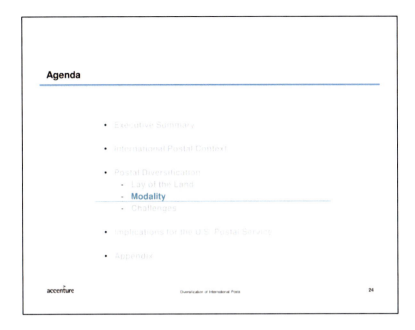

Figure 12-10: Accenture's USPS presentation slide #24

At first glance, the slide #25 (Figure 12-11) looks like a summary node. Given everything we have learned so far, as well as the fact that Accenture has already relied on this proven technique, we should expect to progress sequentially through each of the five platforms – transportation, retail services, mail-related services, emerging services, and government services. A longer presentation (or report) would drill into each of the areas comprising the platforms in depth-order tree traversal fashion. However, as shown in the outline in Figure 12-12, Accenture keeps the platform→area concept broad and instead goes deep with a specific prescription: focus on developing capabilities in one key area at a time. Since Figure 12-12 provides the questions that drive the narrative flow, I'll simply leave it to you to browse the remaining slides #26 to #30 (Figures #13 to #17) in the "Modality" subsection without further explanation.

Figure 12-11: Accenture's USPS presentation slide #25

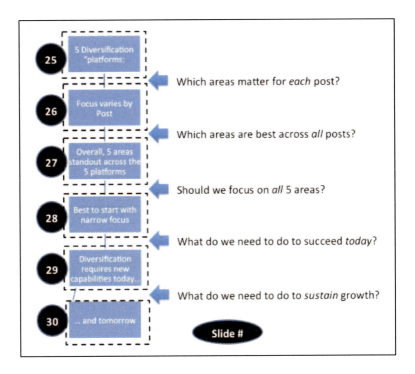

Figure 12-12: Structure of Accenture's USPS "Modality" subsection

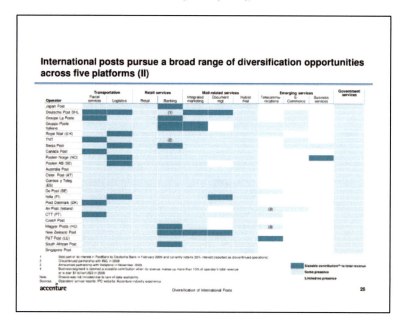

Figure 12-13: Accenture's USPS presentation slide #26

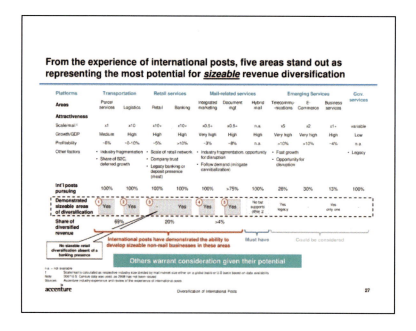

Figure 12-14: Accenture's USPS presentation slide #27

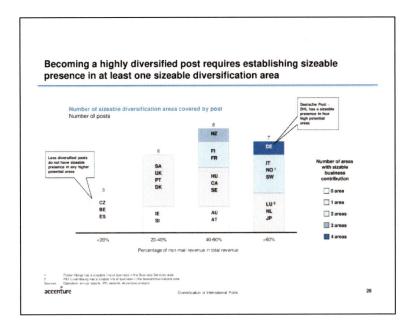

Figure 12-15: Accenture's USPS presentation slide #28

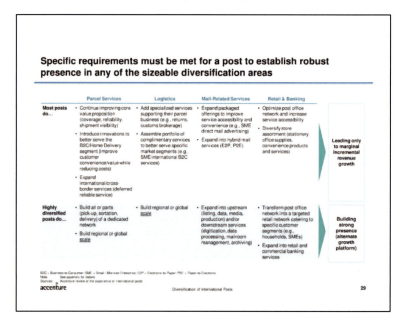

Figure 12-16: Accenture's USPS presentation slide #29

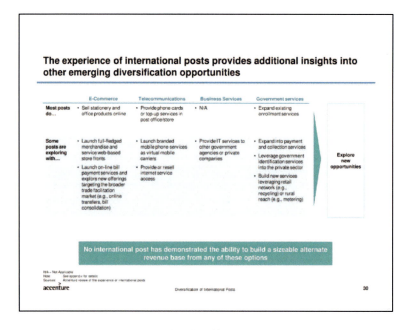

Figure 12-17: Accenture's USPS presentation slide #30

Let's get our bearings in the overall strategic story once more. Accenture's situation section established that international posts face a number of challenges. The first of three opportunity subsections proved diversification is a profitable answer to the challenges and the second subsection established how to diversify. While the end of the second subsection highlighted business-as-usual requirements to succeed at diversification, the third opportunity subsection, ushered in by slide #31 (Figure 12-18), brings structural requirements to the forefront as critical to success.

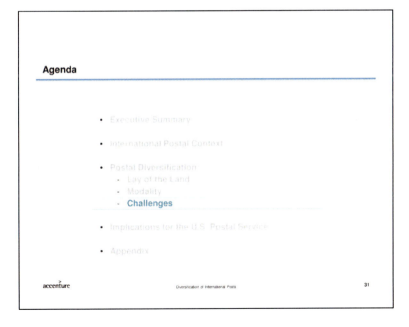

Figure 12-18: Accenture's USPS presentation slide #31

Accenture's presentation returns to the summary node approach beginning with slide #32 (Figure 12-19). This slide sets up the three sub-plot lines including the needs for resources, time, and business model alterations as illustrated by the second level of the outline in Figure 12-20.

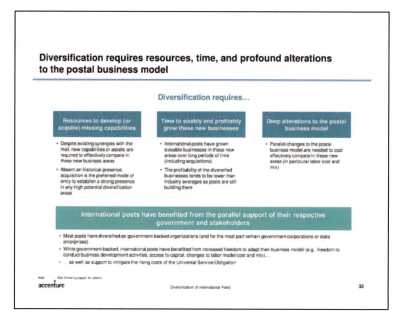

Figure 12-19: Accenture's USPS presentation slide #32

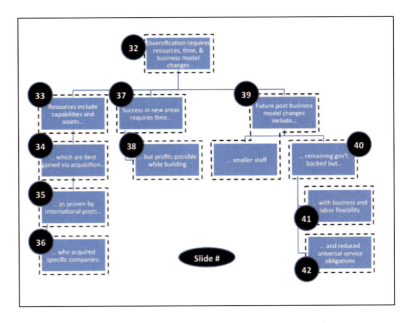

Figure 12-20: Outline of Accenture's USPS "Challenges" subsection

Slide #33 (Figure 12-21) is the start of the first subplot and follows a linear progression into resource needs for new capabilities and assets. The question, "How should we acquire those resources?" is answered by slide #34 (Figure 12-22). The next question, "How many acquisitions are necessary to succeed?," is answered by slide #35 (Figure 12-23). The subplot concludes in slide #36 (Figure 12-24) by answering the question, "What specific companies did leading international posts acquire?"

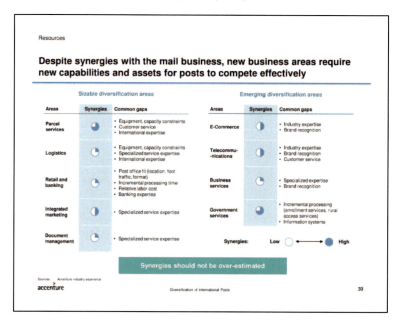

Figure 12-21: Accenture's USPS presentation slide #33

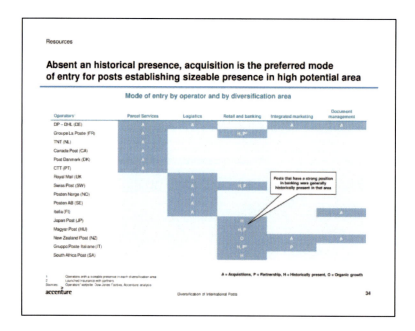

Figure 12-22: Accenture's USPS presentation slide #34

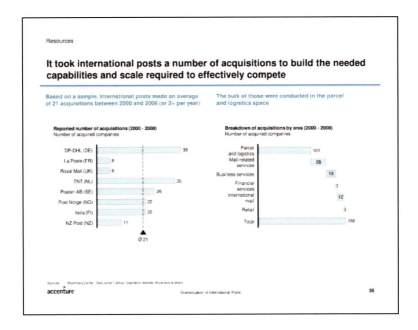

Figure 12-23: Accenture's USPS presentation slide #35

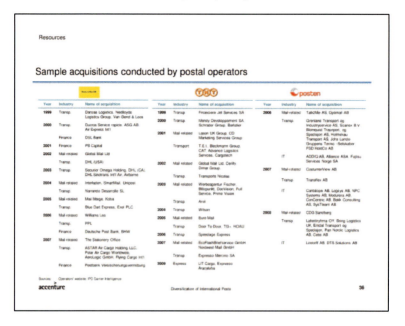

Figure 12-24: Accenture's USPS presentation slide #36

Slide #37 (Figure 12-25) kicks off the second subplot, time. Although spanning only two slides as compared to four, the second subplot is structured as a linear progression just as the first one was. In this case, the first slide proffers Accenture's position that establishing a sizeable presence in non-mail markets will take time. Recall that the USPS is in financial crisis mode. Consequently, one would expect the audience to respond, "But, we don't have time! What can we do generate profit sooner?" Slide #38 (Figure 12-26) answers that question directly – the USPS can expect to generate profit even during the building phase.

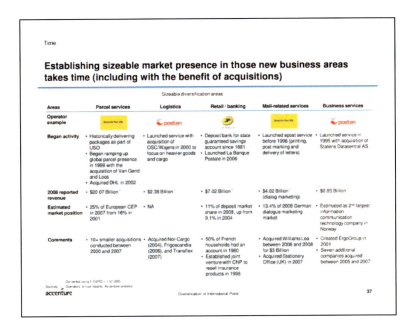

Figure 12-25: Accenture's USPS presentation slide #37

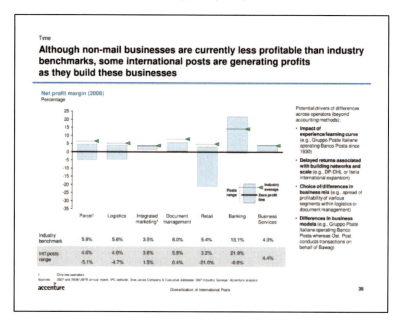

Figure 12-26: Accenture's USPS presentation slide #38

Thus the business model alteration subplot unlike the prior two contains not one but two threads. The first thread is related to staffing and the second related to government considerations. As such, the slide that begins this section *should* serve as a summary node. However, slide #39 (Figure 12-27) takes the unconventional, and I would argue ill-advised, approach of diving right into staffing considerations.

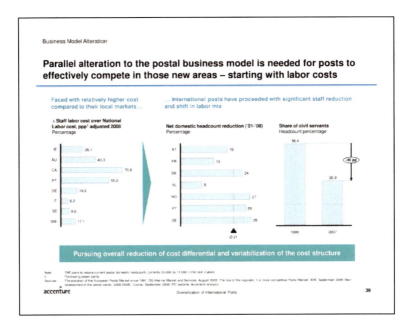

Figure 12-27: Accenture's USPS presentation slide #39

The problem with skipping a summary node for the business model alteration subplot is that slide #40 (Figure 12-28) switches the narrative from staffing to government considerations with no context. Slide #40 (Figure 12-28) contends that posts have successfully diversified without needing to resort to privatization. However, the posts need to have flexibility in adjusting their business model as shown in slide #41 (Figure 12-29) and in relaxing their universal service obligation as shown in slide #42 (Figure 12-30).

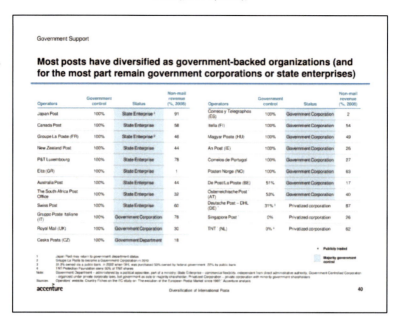

Figure 12-28: Accenture's USPS presentation slide #40

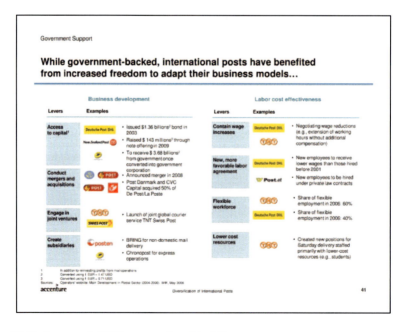

Figure 12-29: Accenture's USPS presentation slide #41

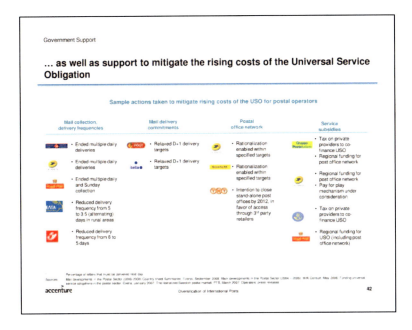

Figure 12-30: Accenture's USPS presentation slide #42

* * * * *

The end of the opportunity section, like the end of any Act II, is the climax of the strategic story. Now that Accenture has identified the opportunity; it is time to find out *how* the USPS can capitalize on it.

Chapter 13

Accenture's USPS Resolution

In this situation-opportunity-resolution presentation, Accenture's first Act explored the profitability crisis facing international posts as a result of loss of relevance, loss of monopoly, and rising costs of universal service obligations. The second act offered diversification into selected non-mail products and services as the best way out of the crisis for posts *in general*. The final act, labeled "Implications for the U.S. Postal Service" in slide #43 (Figure 13-1), describes *how* the USPS *in particular* can capture the opportunity.

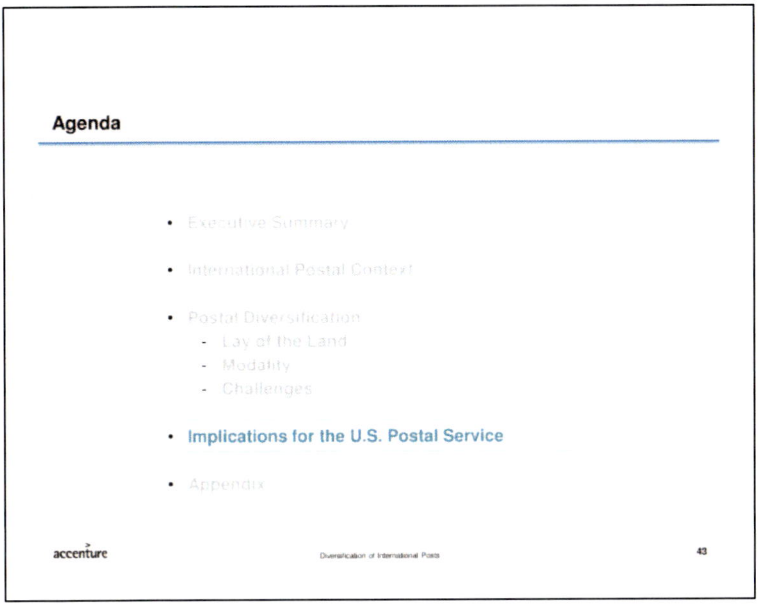

Agenda

- Executive Summary
- International Postal Context
- Postal Diversification
  - Lay of the Land
  - Modality
  - Challenges
- **Implications for the U.S. Postal Service**
- Appendix

accenture   Diversification of International Posts   43

Figure 13-1: Accenture's USPS presentation slide #43

Resolutions are ordinarily very direct – do this, then do that; final acts generally require little in the way of background context because all the characters and sources of tension are already known. However, Accenture's USPS presentation is somewhat unique in that the focus shifts from international posts in the first two sections to the USPS in the third section. Because of that shift we need to know a little about what is going on with the USPS in order to accept that the diversification resolution is the correct one for the organization.

We already know that the best way to apply a set of recommendations to a new context using strategic storytelling principles is to use the situation-complication-resolution format! This is precisely what Accenture does when they embed a complete

SCR as the third act. It is also unusual since focus shifts at the end of a story are (and should be) rare, but here it works.

The mini-situation begins on slide #44 (Figure 13-2) which serves as the now very familiar summary node slide. The USPS is in a very unfavorable position due to low diversification and declining mail volumes. Slide #45 (Figure 13-3) proves the low diversification point and slide #46 (Figure 13-4) proves the declining mail volumes point.

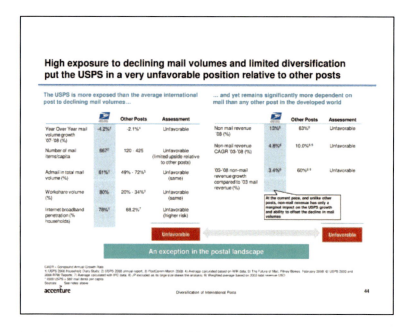

Figure 13-2: Accenture's USPS presentation slide #44

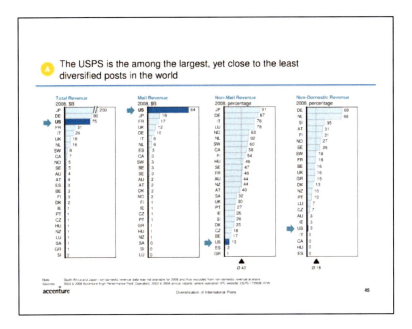

Figure 13-3: Accenture's USPS presentation slide #45

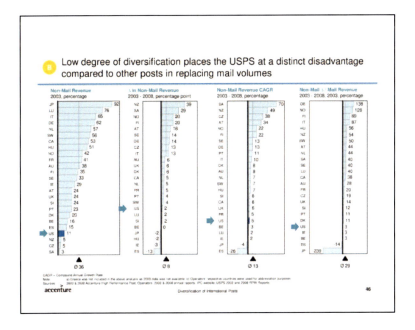

Figure 13-4: Accenture's USPS presentation slide #46

The mini-complication is presented in its entirety on slide #47 (Figure 13-5). To remain self-funding, the USPS needs to offset a massive, $7.8 billion loss, spun euphemistically as a "profit shortfall."

From a storytelling standpoint, all Accenture needed to share on this slide are the near-term challenges facing the USPS. Applying the SCR framework, it is too early to discuss diversification and structural change as solutions. Moreover, I would eliminate the hyperbolic comparisons to "creating 13 Fortune 500 companies" and "building an e-commerce business 8x the size of Amazon.com." In addition, everything we know so far is about international posts. So, why bring in new "characters" in the form of other, non-governmental industries? If music publishing, video rental, and so on were the source of diversification best practices most applicable to postal services, then we should have heard a lot more about that before.

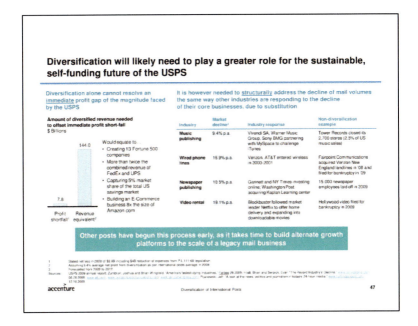

Figure 13-5: Accenture's USPS presentation slide #47

After a questionably designed mini-complication, Accenture's USPS presentation ends on a strong note with the mini-resolution in slide #48 (Figure 13-6). The four actions the USPS must take to restore profitability through non-mail diversification mirror the international post best practices enumerated in the opportunity section.

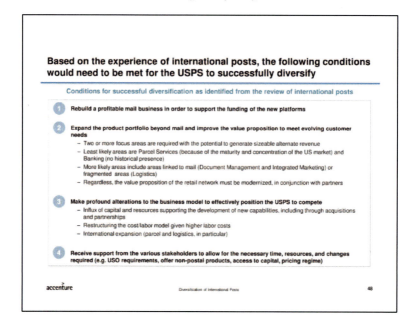

Figure 13-6: Accenture's USPS presentation slide #48

Chapter 14

The Pilot-Results-Scale Framework

Before exploring the visual component of strategic storytelling, you need to consider one more strategic storytelling framework, pilot-results-scale (PRS). As you might have guessed, this is simply another variation on SCR where the pilot (or small test) is the situation, the results of the pilot are the complication, and the recommendation to scale-up is, well, the recommendation.

Recall Accenture's ultimate recommendation on slide #48 (Figure 13-6) that the USPS is likely to be most successful with diversification into either mail-related services (document management, integrated marketing, and logistics. By way of further reminder, mail-related services on slide #25 (Figure 12-11) include document digitization, archiving, printing, customer response management, and a range of related services. Logistics includes warehousing, freight forwarding, and so on.

Imagine for a moment the *expected* investment of time, money, and energy, as well as the *expected* return on investment are identical for the mail-related services market and the logistics market.

Moreover, imagine the USPS could only handle one major non-mail diversification initiative at a time. In the old days, decision makers in this situation would have "gone with their gut" and chosen the one that "felt right." Armies of people and truckloads of money would have been invested in building a comprehensive business plan and then building out massive infrastructure. While that still happens occasionally, most of the business world is rapidly moving toward lean innovation techniques.

While there are some outstanding books on the topic (including my favorite, <u>The Four Steps to the Epiphany</u> by Steve Blank), I'll grossly simplify the whole process down to three steps for designing a minimum viable product, testing it with real customers who have paid real money, and integrating what you learn into the next design. "Piloting" is the simple name for this rinse-and-repeat process. Stated another way, the days of building the whole enchilada and seeing if they will come are over. The new era of building a prototype just good enough to excite early adopters and scale up through rapid iteration is here.

Getting back to our hypothetical scenario, imagine the USPS embraced lean innovation and created two project teams, one tasked with exploring mail-related services and one tasked with exploring logistics. Taking just one as an example, the non-mail services team brings an SCR to persuade USPS leadership to approve a pilot as follows:

- Situation: We, the USPS, are facing a financial crisis. Accenture has identified mail-related services as a profitable area for non-mail diversification. Moreover, we are highly likely to succeed because of synergies with our existing assets and capabilities. At scale, we expect to make $(…) per year at a (…) times return on investment.

- Complication: "Mail-related services" is a broad category including but not limited to integrated marketing and document management. We have hypotheses about the sub-services our potential customers value and about the return on investment on those sub-services, but possess no first-hand experience.

- Resolution: We propose a pilot to answer the following open questions (…) with the following scope (…) over the following timeframe (…) and with the following human and financial resources (…). The pilot will be judged a success if we achieve the following on our key performance indicators (…).

The pilot-results-scale strategic story comes into play *after* the pilot is complete. Act I is a reminder – We conducted a pilot to answer the following open questions… Act II shares the results of the pilot. Rarely do the results fully confirm or fully refute the hypotheses you set out to test. More frequently you will end up confirming a few things, refuting a few others, and discovering valuable new insights. Finally, Act III is a request for more time, money, and energy to scale the pilot either up another notch or to a full-scale line of business. Just as the SCR request to pilot, the PRS request to scale should come with a solid business case detailing scope, timeframe, resources, expected return on investment, and key performance indicators.

Finally, note the PRS framework can be generalized to serve as a template for any project status update. Too often, professionals deliver bland updates to their superiors and wonder why praise, raises, and promotions are not forthcoming. Valuable employees do more than update or inform, they lead with the overarching business objective and a review of what they set out to do. They then share their results without sugar-coating or hiding anything. Finally, they recommend a plan for what to do next.

Section 2:
Data-Driven Design

Chapter 15

To Slide or Not to Slide

Before diving into the nitty-gritty of the slide-design techniques that support strategic storytelling, let's pause for one chapter to consider when and how to use slides.

Just as persuasive content structure traces to a one-time McKinsey employee, so too does persuasive content design. While his mentor Barbara Minto focused on structure, Gene Zelazny concentrated on design and delivery. More than 50 years after they met, they still run in these two distinct lanes. Mr. Zelazny's core concepts for the visual display of quantitative information remain keenly relevant even though his books were published more than a decade ago.

Tip 38: Use slides only when they accelerate decision-making

While this tip may seem obvious, I find that business people create slides every time they deliver a presentation without taking the time to consider whether or not slides accelerate decision-making. The urge to "build a PowerPoint deck" is so strongly ingrained that I think people have lost, or never developed in the first place, the ability to present without technical accompaniment or even understand that there are times when slides do more harm than good. From the point of view of the speaker, the only outcome that matters in a persuasive business presentation is approval to implement a recommendation. (Yes, the decision to take a different and better course of action constitutes success, too.) If slides help you get to "yes," use them. If not, don't.

When do slides hurt? I can think of at least three instances, starting with engaging a hostile audience due to risk aversion or the all-too-common personality conflict. If you put slides in front of skeptics, they will assume a whole range of negative motivations including the possibility that you do not care for their input or that you want to claim all the credit for the ultimate results. For coworkers, especially peers, to support an initiative, they must be invested from the earliest stages of a project and that investment begins with dialogue, not input on slides.

Slides are a barrier not only to collaborating with a hostile audience, but also to brainstorming with a friendly one. Guiding the *entire* ideation process with slides risks closing people's minds, the second instance of slides doing more harm than good.

There are three appropriate uses for slides during a brainstorming session:

- The first is to clearly establish the problem you want solved. The problem definition may include the ultimate objective as well as any guiding principles or constraints in effect. Any debate over which problem to solve and whether it is worth solving to begin with should be resolved long before you assemble a group of people in a room. You may go so far as to establish the current state (situation) and the desired state (opportunity) so that ideation can focus on bridging the gap (resolution).

- The second is to share the procedure to be used for the brainstorming session, including any ground rules.
- The third is for on-the-fly capture of ideas. It does not matter whether the meeting scribe captures information electronically, on whiteboards, or giant pieces of paper stuck to the wall, the point is to give the audience the visual confirmation it needs to confirm its input matters.

The third instance of when the excessive use of slides can do more harm than good is during corporate training. Since this book is about persuading higher-ups to approve recommendations packaged as strategic stories, corporate training is beyond the scope of this book so I cannot go into too much depth about it, however, I will say that the best framework I have seen for training is to take students through the "see one, do one, teach one" cycle. Slides are fine during the "see one" phase, but should be avoided during the other two phases, except perhaps to set-up the exercise. As in the collaboration and brainstorming cases, training success demands dialogue.

The situation-complication-resolution framework, as well as the variations I have discussed, is a persuasive concept based on strategic storytelling that works in any form of communication including conversations, slide-less presentations, presentations with slides, emails, written reports, and so on. Choose the right medium for the message based on your objective and the best way to engage your specific audience.

Tip 39: The larger the audience, the simpler the slides

Even in the many instances where slides have the potential to accelerate decision-making, many speakers make the mistake of designing slides that are far too densely packed with content. Sometimes this happens because the speaker wants to show off how much they know and the vast amount of work done. Other times, speakers create dense slides that function as speaker notes. Either reason is poor; slides must be designed as simply as possible in service of the audience.

Notice that I added "in service of the audience." When seeking to persuade a highly technical, detail oriented decision maker one-on-one, then extremely dense slides are likely the best choice. On the other hand, when delivering a keynote address to thousands, then slides with vivid, full-screen photographs are a suitable choice.

In the forthcoming chapters, I will focus on designing slides for the typical business audience of five to fifteen people, give or take a few on either end. For such groups, slides with clear titles supported by light to moderate amounts of information are appropriate and effective.

Tip 40 : The content in the body of the slide must unambiguously prove the slide title

To prove "unprecedented losses" as shown in slide #2 (Figure 15-1), McKinsey appropriately included a chart with ten-years of financial history plus the expected loss in the current year. A column of text addressing "Key drivers" for the losses supplements the chart. Indeed, four consecutive years of multi-billion dollar losses qualifies as unprecedented, though a stickler would want proof this never happened in the long history of the USPS. An extreme stickler would want to see that greater losses had not been experienced by other national postal services, either.

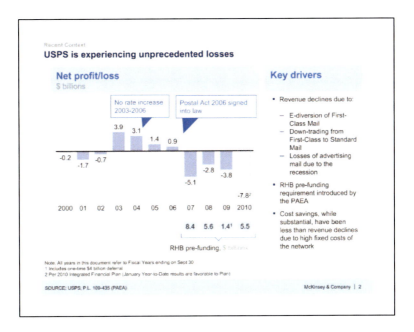

Figure 15-1: McKinsey's USPS presentation slide #2

Tip 41: Match the design treatment in the slide body to the message in the title

To support a given message, a speaker can draw from a range of design treatments, including: text, graphs, tables, diagrams, and images. Though each of these five treatments has infinite variations, each form typically serves a specific function. Text is best suited for drawing attention to key insights. Graphs convey time-series trends, composition (including rank and share), distribution, and correlation. Tables are an alternative to graphs when precision is required, the quantity of data is minimal, or when data is non-numeric. Diagrams illustrate processes and relationships. Finally, images function in opposite ways. Either they pair nicely with emotional speeches, or they convey extremely complex, often technical, information that would otherwise take a thousand words to explain (just imagine assembling furniture using an instruction manual without images).

Tip 42: Design each slide so that it can be covered in three minutes or less

Presentation design software makes it easy to include multiple design treatments on a single slide. If you find yourself adding multiple instances of one treatment or mixing treatments (excepting text) on a single slide, there is a good chance you are loading too much on it and should consider presenting the information in two or more slides. It takes no more, and possibly even less, time to present the same content spread across multiple slides as it does to review all of the content on a single slide. Your audience will thank you for this because slide changes create energy by engaging the visual cortex and signaling progress toward the end.

Perhaps the best test of whether you have too much content on a slide is if it takes you more than three minutes to deliver what is on it. Most of the business meetings I attend range from thirty minutes to one hour. To ensure an on-time ending, I recommend creating enough slides to fill twenty-five minutes of content for a thirty-minute meeting and fifty minutes of content for an hour-long meeting. The extra time serves as a buffer for latecomers on the front end, for summarizing actions and decisions on the back end, and for handling questions. Also, to my knowledge, no one has ever been fired for chronically ending meetings early. Applying the three-minute-per-slide rule-of-thumb, creates at most 8 content rich slides for a half-hour meeting and 16 for a one-hour meeting. If you tend to linger on title slides, agenda slides, and divider slides, a practice I do not recommend, then include them in your count, as well.

Tip 43: Use animation sparingly (if at all)

In addition to making content overload too easy to perpetrate, presentation design software in the wrong hands can allow for the triumph of style over substance. Specifically, speakers should use builds and slide transitions sparingly if at all.

Builds reveal slide content progressively either "on click" or after a user-specified time delay. One could simulate a build by adding content one piece at a time to a sequence of slides, but that poses the challenge of keeping everything identical during updates and edits.

In special circumstances, builds aid strategic storytelling. For instance, imagine you wanted to show a four-step process leading to a single outcome. If each step requires detailed explanation, it behooves you to use a build. I can think of several other reasonably good opportunities to use builds, including but not limited to:

- Starting with a cause and then revealing its effect
- Showing the history of a time-series and then adding a forecast

- Showing the full slide content and then adding transition question text at the bottom (this is most useful when the slide content triggers simultaneous questions or when the question is not obvious)

My biggest objection to builds is that they draw attention away from the speaker every time content is revealed. In most circumstances, it is better to show all of the content, let people mentally process it, and then allow time for their eyes to shift back to you.

Builds have other disadvantages. First, they delay discussion since listeners, out of respect for the speaker, wait for all of the content to appear. Second, by allowing content to appear and disappear, builds allow designers to layer content. If your slide does not look good when all content elements are shown, you are probably abusing the build feature.

Just as builds draw attention away from speakers, so too do animated slide transitions. As a rule, I never use them. They are particularly unprofessional in smaller business meetings, precisely the type in which you are most likely to find yourself. If you must use a slide transition, keep it subtle and short. From-right wipes, where the new slide covers the old, is the best choice. Smooth fades, where the new slide appears while the old slide disappears, is also an acceptable alternative. Avoid special variations on these two transitions, as well as all other transition types, unless you are a trained professional. It is also important to keep transitions to a half-second; less than that is too abrupt and more is boring. Finally, eschew sounds at transitions unless you are in second grade and the whole point is to dazzle the other kids with your PowerPoint prowess.

Tip 44: Lay out body content from left-to-right and top-to-bottom

Look closely at dramatic storytelling and you will find three-part narrative structures repeated like fractals. The overall story has a beginning (Act I), middle (Act II), and end Act III). Each act has a beginning, middle, and end, too. The main difference between the overall story and an individual act is that tension is left unresolved at the end of Act I and Act II. Next, each Act is made up of (typically) five to ten sequences and each sequence contains a number of scenes. And, you guessed it, sequences and scenes have their own three-part structures.

I bring all this up because these same principles apply to presentation design. A strategic story has three parts: the situation, the complication, and the resolution – usually in that order. Each part tells its own partial story with tension left unresolved at the end of the situation and the complication. Similarly, each slide needs to be viewed as a scene and should tell a story all its own.

Laying a story on a slide from left-to-right and top-to-bottom is the style that mirrors the manner in which English language speakers read. McKinsey placed the financial history chart as the first element in the upper left because it is the strongest proof of unprecedented losses and because it is the beginning of the story the slides reveal.

Tip 45: Maintain strict design consistency

In order to effectively execute with the form over function theme I keep harping on, strive to maintain strict design consistency. From slide to slide, stick with the same:

- Fonts, inclusive of type, slide, and color
- Alignment and placement of elements such as titles, charts, and text boxes
- Colors and textures used in images, charts, etc.

Every design element - colors, fonts, etc. – has meaning. Sometimes these meanings are culturally predetermined, such as the color red signaling danger in Western cultures and good fortune in Eastern cultures. More often, however, design elements take on their own meaning from the first time you use them. For instance, when you show a revenue trend line using a solid black line for historical numbers and a dashed grey line for forecasted values, your audience subconsciously expects a consistent treatment in all future trend line graphs. If you change the formatting, or worse reverse it, you slow comprehension.

* * * * *

Before moving on to best practices for using text in strategic stories, I offer one more caveat. The ease of use and bells and whistles in presentation design software makes it very easy to over-design. Keep your story front-and-center and remember that great design is best when it is not noticed.

Chapter 16

Text

Text is the most used and most abused design treatment ven in data-driven presentations. Fortunately, McKinsey, BCG, and Accenture applied a full array of best practices that you can leverage in your own strategic stories. In this chapter we will start with a simple bulleted list and progress toward more creatively designed text slides. Through it all, bear in mind that dazzling design is only valuable insofar as it helps listeners make informed decisions.

Tip 46 : Maximize contrast between the text and the background

The first thing to notice about Accenture's slide #7 (Figure 16-1) is the degree to which the text stands out against the background. Black text on a white background is so familiar that we do not even think of it as a design choice. Yet, it is a choice; a choice that connotes neutrality and simplicity.

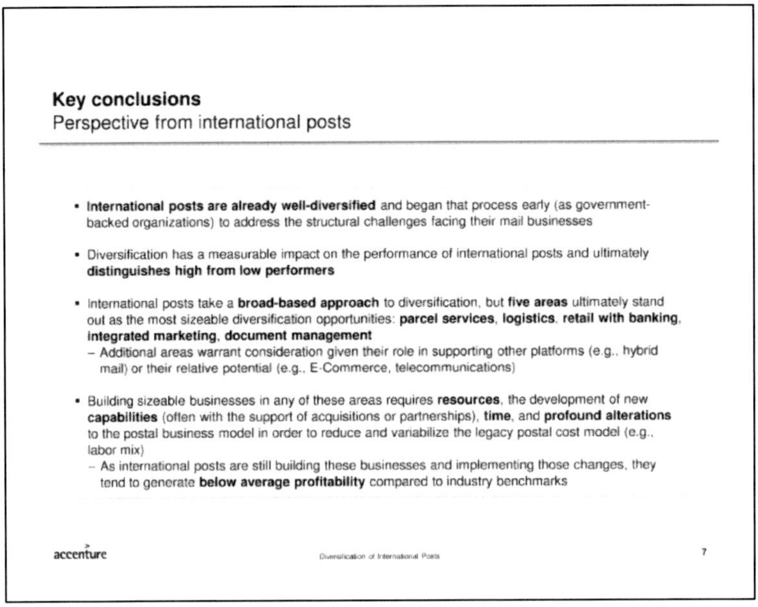

> **Key conclusions**
> Perspective from international posts
>
> - **International posts are already well-diversified** and began that process early (as government-backed organizations) to address the structural challenges facing their mail businesses
> - Diversification has a measurable impact on the performance of international posts and ultimately **distinguishes high from low performers**
> - International posts take a **broad-based approach** to diversification, but **five areas** ultimately stand out as the most sizeable diversification opportunities: **parcel services, logistics, retail with banking, integrated marketing, document management**
>   - Additional areas warrant consideration given their role in supporting other platforms (e.g., hybrid mail) or their relative potential (e.g., E-Commerce, telecommunications)
> - Building sizeable businesses in any of these areas requires **resources**, the development of new **capabilities** (often with the support of acquisitions or partnerships), **time**, and **profound alterations** to the postal business model in order to reduce and variabilize the legacy postal cost model (e.g., labor mix)
>   - As international posts are still building these businesses and implementing those changes, they tend to generate **below average profitability** compared to industry benchmarks
>
> accenture   Diversification of International Posts   7

Figure 16-1: Accenture's USPS presentation slide #7

White text on a black background has just as much contrast as the reverse, as shown in Figure 16-2. However, white text is harder to read. Even the bold "International posts are already well-diversified" stands out much better in black text than in white. Consequently, white text on a dark background should be reserved for instances when you want to draw attention, as when using labels or titles. Recall BCG's presentation in which the orange slide titles worked nicely against the dark green background, but the white bullet text in the body against the same background ultimately grew tiresome.

> - **International posts are already well-diversified** and began that process early (as government-backed organizations) to address the structural challenges facing their mail businesses

Figure 16-2: First bullet from Accenture slide #7, text and background colors reversed

Tip 47: Use solid colors for slide backgrounds

While we are on the subject of effective backgrounds, notice that Accenture's slide #7 (Figure 16-1) has a solid background. Any pattern or image in the background, no matter how subtle, draws the reader's eye away from the text and makes it less readable. If a textured background has critical meaning, by all means use it, but if it is purely decorative eliminate it. Once again, I'm going to fault BCG – this time for embedding its company logo in a massive font into the background of every slide. The USPS paid for this presentation to address its plight, so this seems an inappropriate design choice, conveying no small amount of hubris. In contrast, Accenture placed a diminutive version of its logo in the slide footer, a best practice of maximizing readability while gently reminding the reader of the slide's creator. The bottom right and the bottom left are the subtlest locations to place a logo. (Note: Footers should also include page numbers, unless you are delivering a keynote presentation.)

Tip 48: Use large, standard fonts

Unless you are an expert designer, use exactly two standard fonts in your presentation, one for slide titles and one for body text.

Slide titles, critical as they are, demand attention in a large, bold, high-contrast, sans-serif font. Standard sans-serif fonts like Ariel, Helvetica, and Century Gothic lack the little tails that help connect letters. Throughout the USPS presentation, Accenture used standard capitalization for slide titles. I prefer title capitalization ("Key Conclusions" instead of "Key conclusions"), but either stylistic treatment will do. Since slide titles should be stated as complete sentences, they may span up to two lines.

Body text should be in a more readable serif font since there is usually much more of it compared to title text. Standard serif fonts include Times New Roman and Georgia.

Use fonts large enough to be read. If you project your presentation on a screen, words must be legible to people seated in the back of the room. In most cases, this means title text of at least 36 point and body text of at least 24 point. Go as large as possible while maintaining the roughly 12-point delta between the two. Accenture appears to have dipped below this font size considered the minimum for projected presentations. Giving the firm the benefit of the doubt, perhaps Accenture's presentation is really a report intended for close reading and, therefore, warrants this smaller size font.

Tip 49: Keep text short

The opening bullet in Accenture's slide #7 (Figure 16-1) is much easier to read than the final bullet. The reason, obviously, is length;

the initial bullet point spans two lines of text as compared to the closing bullet's four lines, six if you include the sub-bullet.

But, brevity is not the only reason the first bullet is easier to read, because it also "leads with the lead" placing the most important information at the front of the text. Even though the other three bullets use boldface type to pull out keywords, none are as easy to comprehend as the first bullet point.

As complete sentences, all of the bullets follow the best practice of applying parallel construction, however complete sentences are more suitable for reading, not presenting to an audience.

Tip 50: Apply a consistent format to your slide header

To uncover other best practices for using text in strategic stories, let's turn to McKinsey's slide #24 (Figure 16-3). McKinsey presentation slide headers use one or more of the following three elements, including: section titles, slide titles, and slide headlines.

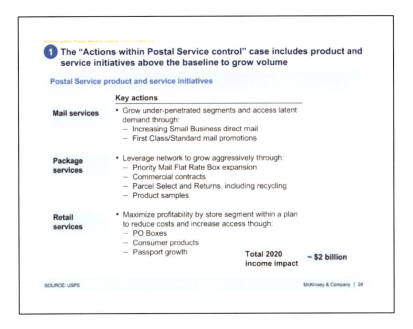

Figure 16-3: McKinsey USPS presentation slide #24

The first element is the section title, here. This optional element is most useful when used in longer presentations to help the audience stay focused and not lose track of where you are in the story. If you use a section title, allow it to drift into the background by giving it a very light treatment as McKinsey did with "Actions within Postal Service control: Productivity" in a small, light-orange font.

McKinsey violates the rule of *total* consistency by varying the color of the section title as the story progresses. Breaking a rule is always acceptable when it helps the audience follow the story as it did in this presentation. The color shifts even suit the emotional tone of the content. The situation section carries the light-grey section title "Recent Context" conveying factual and emotional neutrality. The complication section carries the red section title "Base Case" conveying trouble. The resolution section title starts with light-orange for "Actions within Postal Service control" signaling that attention is required, then shifts to green for "Fundamental Change" underscoring that these final actions will restore the USPS to full financial health.

The second element is the slide title, sometimes referred to as a lead. This element is required as it contains the primary information content in the slide and carries the narrative. In McKinsey's slide #24 (Figure 16-3), the title is "The 'Actions within Postal Service control' case includes product and service initiatives above the baseline to grow volume." I'll cover more on the content of well-articulated slide titles in the following tip.

The third element is the headline. These are optionally found in slide headers below the title and are complete sentences that provide an additional level of detail. While not found in this presentation, they are common in McKinsey presentations. Slide headlines, being less important than slide titles, are usually in moderately smaller, slightly lower contrast fonts.

This is a good place to mention that you do not necessarily need to have a slide header. Used sparingly, slides lacking headers draw attention to themselves. Although rare in everyday business presentations, slides with large images are more powerful when they do not contain headers. Dramatic slides with only a few words of text do not need headers either.

Tip 51: Craft each slide title as a "so-what"

Each slide title, like the title of the presentation, should reflect a "so-what" rather than a "what." In the case of this slide, an inferior "what" title would be "Product and Service Initiatives." Though a bit long, McKinsey's "The 'Actions within Postal Service control' case includes product and service initiatives above the baseline to grow volume" is a well-crafted "so-what."

One of the guiding principles in creating strategic business stories is having your audience perform as little cognitive work as possible. Do not make them figure out what you are trying to say; instead use a "so-what" title to tell them what you are saying. That way, individuals can focus all their mental energy on making a decision. If you are pinched for time, you can read through the titles only, one after the other, and still give the complete picture – a nice side benefit!

In general, I do not recommend using questions as slide titles since they make the audience do the work. The actual title is superior to "What actions within USPS control can increase volume?" One reasonable exception is asking a question in the title one slide and then answering it in the title of the next one, but use this technique sparingly.

A better alternative is to span a title across multiple slides using ellipses. For instance, "USPS should pursue volume boosting initiatives…" followed on the next slide by "… by taking critical actions leading to ~$2 billion of incremental net income in 2020." This approach helps a presentation feel more like a cohesive story.

Tip 52: Convert bullet lists into columns

By labeling and grouping the key actions, McKinsey's slide #24 (Figure 16-3) is visually more interesting than Accenture's slide #7 (Figure 16-1), despite the blue box surrounding the latter's standard vertical list. Accenture gains back the upper hand in slide #19 (Figure 16-4) by converting into columns information that otherwise could have been represented as a bland list. This technique is called "chunking" and was taught to me by presentation design guru Nolan Haims.

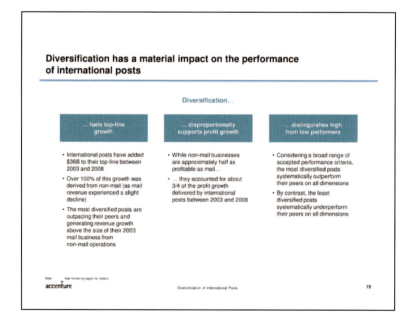

Figure 16-4: Accenture's USPS opportunity slide #19

In the hands of an expert designer, "chunking" is quite elegant with blocks of text placed creatively rather than simply in boring rows or columns. While not reaching the level of artistic use of text one would find in a professionally designed advertisement, McKinsey's slide #10 (Figure 16-5) adds additional visual variety through the use of chunking. Reading the slide from outside in, there are four chunks of text, one each for volume, price, USO obligation, and workforce costs laid-out in a grid. Next, notice that each chunk has its own "so-what" – volume is… declining steadily; price is… rising but capped; and so on. Finally, the innermost label summarizes the confluence of the four trends. This is an effective and visually pleasing format to convey the impact of multiple forces on a business and anyone can design it.

Figure 16-5: McKinsey USPS presentation slide #10

Tip 53: Use real quotes that you obtained directly

Let's now turn our attention to how to best use quotes in business presentations. Most problem solving processes that culminate in strategic storytelling include qualitative interviews of key stakeholders, including customers, suppliers, fellow employees, etc. Among the three management-consulting firms, only BCG gets credit for including such quotes in its presentation. In BCG's slide #13 (Figure 16-6), all five quotes prove the title "Senders tell us that they see their use of mail declining sharply." Moreover, all sources appear highly credible.

Figure 16-6: BCG's USPS presentation slide #13

Designers have at least three options when including quotes in a strategic story. The first, as illustrated in BCG's slide #13 (Figure 16-6), is the overwhelming force approach. The sheer volume of diverse, highly credible sources quoted means the audience can get the message without reading every quote in detail. The second option is to add contrast to one of the quotes most representative of the group. The third and most radical option is to show *only* the most representative quote. Nine times out of ten, I follow the third approach, relying on the principle that less is more, even with extremely analytical decision-makers; I would rather increase the odds that my audience reads one powerful quote than overwhelm them with volume.

Finally, apply the highest ethical standards to quote selection. If you interview enough people, somebody is bound to make the perfect statement to support the argument you want to make, but if that one statement is an aberration you have a duty to disregard it as an outlier and instead share a quote supporting the majority opinion. Additionally, if you show multiple quotes representing different, possibly conflicting, findings, ensure the physical space occupied by quotes supporting each finding matches the prevalence of each type of statement across all interviews.

* * * * *

The source material I drew from for this chapter was extremely text-dense because all three presentations were designed for a reader to comprehend even in the absence of an expert speaker. Most business presentations do not need to "travel" in this manner and should have significantly less text per slide than any of the examples in this chapter.

Fortunately, the examples graphically involved in the next chapter offer ready-to-adopt templates for any data-driven presentation.

Chapter 17

Graphs

The phrase "data-driven storytelling" immediately conjures visions of graphs dancing across a screen. In this chapter, we will explore the following types of graphs: trend, composition (including rank and share), distribution, and correlation. Along the way, I will interweave general graph design practices as we encounter them.

Tip 54: Use column charts for trend data with up to ten values

After framing its story with a title slide and an agenda slide, McKinsey immediately turned to trend data (also referred to as time-series data) in slide #2 (Figure 17-1) to establish the USPS's situational context. Although McKinsey could prove the slide title message of unprecedented losses with one of the other treatment types, it is reasonably safe to say that a column chart representing the trend of financial performance over time is the most compelling choice.

With a limited time-series of around ten values, a column chart (also known as a vertical bar chart) is most effective. Column charts are elegant and easy to read as long as the columns and labels are not squeezed too closely together.

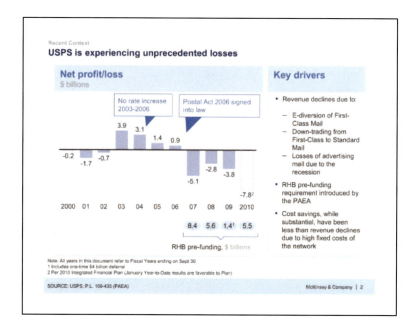

Figure 17-1: McKinsey's USPS presentation slide #2

McKinsey pushed the upper boundary with eleven data points in the trend chart in slide #2 (Figure 17-1). In order to legibly squeeze in that number of values, the designers took the fairly unusual, though acceptable, step of removing the leading "20" from the x-axis labels for the years 2001 to 2009.

Tip 55: Title graphs with a "what" rather than a "so-what"

My recommendation for using a "so-what" to title the overall presentation and each slide can apply to many different types of titles, however graph titles are not one of them. Graph titles should merely explain the function of the graph because it is the visual representation that matters.

The best practice for titling graph titles is to describe the y-axis followed by the x-axis. In a trend chart, "y over time" or "y versus x" is sufficient. In other types of charts, good choices include, "Dependence of y on x," "Relationship between y and x," and "Comparison of y across x."

Given this best practice, why didn't McKinsey label the trend chart in Figure x "Net profit/loss over time"? While the presentation designer certainly could have, minimalism trumps all else in slide design. Since it is obvious the x-axis is time, dropping "over time" is a reasonable choice.

Tip 56: Remove all unnecessary elements from graphs

Compare the net profit/loss chart McKinsey actually designed to the one in Figure 17-2. The actual version is much more professional because it removes all the unnecessary elements.

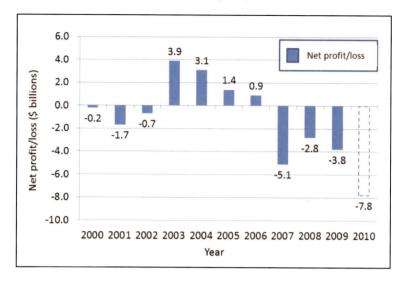

Figure 17-2: Net profit/loss trend chart with too many graphical elements

While there is no strict definition of "necessary," consider the elements that McKinsey removed in order to apply the design principles of minimalism, clarity, and low audience cognitive load. By removing unnecessary elements, the designer created whitespace for information rich annotations. First, the y-axis label disappears since it is explained in the title. Second, the vertical y-axis and its horizontal grid lines are removed as profit values are provided above and below the columns. Third, the x-axis label is deleted as it is clear the values are years, a rare exception to the best practice of labeling each axis with its units of measure. The horizontal x-axis itself remains because there are positive and negative profit values and it is useful to know where zero is; however, the x-axis tick marks are removed since white-space is sufficient to separate each bar. Fourth, the legend vanished as there is only one category of values.

Tip 57: Use chart annotations in the body of a slide to explain critical inflections

The net profit and loss chart contains three annotations, including two call-outs and one embedded "micro" table, to explain critical inflections in the data.

From 2002 to 2003, the USPS shifted from a loss of $0.7 billion to a profit of $3.9 billion. Any reasonable observer would want to know why, as that root cause might offer a solution to the organization's current woes. The annotation "No rate increase 2003-2006" does little to explain the positive shift in 2003, though perhaps it addresses the declining profits through 2006. As such, I find this call out ambiguous and would replace it.

The call-out labeled "Postal Act 2006 signed into law" and the embedded "RHB pre-funding" table work together to explain the losses commencing in 2007. The Postal Accountability and Enhancement Act (PAEA) of 2006 called for pre-funding of retirement health benefits (RHB); as the embedded table reveals, these contributions are a significant root cause of subsequent losses.

As a final note on this topic, I recommend numbering annotations in order to guide the audience through the flow of your story. This practice is especially critical if you need annotations read in any order other than left-to-right or top-to-bottom.

Tip 58: Apply high contrast to chart data that directly supports the slide title

The net profit/loss chart applies uniform formatting to all columns (except the 2010 forecast with which we will deal in the next tip). To reinforce the header, the slide designer might have shaded the large losses incurred between 2007 and 2010 with a different, perhaps dark red, color.

Designers typically apply high contrast to just a single element in a chart. In addition to using a more dramatic color, other options to draw the viewer's eye include arrows and enclosures (for instance, putting a rectangular outline around a column).

Tip 59: Use a more subtle treatment for forecast data

When a trend chart contains a mix of actual and forecast data, use a more subtle treatment on the forecast data to indicate that it is an estimate. McKinsey's slide #2 (Figure 17-1) uses a dashed, light blue rectangle for this and even goes one step further by including a footnote regarding the source of the data.

Tip 60: Footnote sources, critical assumptions, and details too granular for the body of the slide

Footnote all sources to increase the credibility of the data. This practice also benefits you and your team when you quality check your numbers.

When chart data is obtained through quantitative modeling rather than direct measurement, document critical assumptions in the footnotes. To believe your estimates, audiences will want to know that your assumptions are reasonably conservative.

At times, an audience member may question at a deeper level of granularity than what you show on a slide or on the subsequent slide. To help you answer this type of question, place granular details in a footnote. For instance, in the net profit/loss chart, you might expect a question on the two components of profit, revenues and costs. If your data is too detailed for a footnote, include it in an appendix slide at the end of your presentation.

Tip 61: Design stacked column charts to show an overall trend and its components

The stacked column chart in McKinsey's slide #6 (Figure 17-3) is a convenient way to show an overall trend and its composition. The overall, highly volatile trend is as discernable as it would be if the components were not broken out.

Showing any extra information comes at a cost. Besides making out the overall trend, the audience can accurately interpret only the trend in the component adjoining the axis. Hence, selecting which component to place where is an important design decision. Why did McKinsey put "Employer premiums" and not "PAEA scheduled pre-funding requirement" against the x-axis? Because doing so shows regular employer premiums are small and stable as compared to the pre-funding requirement.

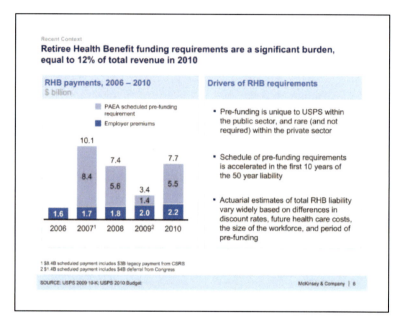

Figure 17-3: McKinsey USPS presentation slide #6

When reading the trend in both components simultaneously is important, then the clustered column chart shown in Figure 17-4 is the best choice. This change, too, comes with a cost – gaining the ability to discern both trends sacrifices the ability to see the overall trend. There is no right or wrong; choose the style based on the message you want to convey.

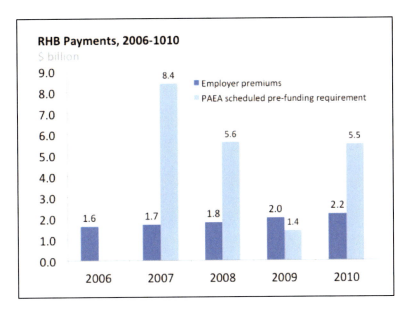

Figure 17-4: Graph from McKinsey slide #6 converted to clustered column style

In a column chart, the columns for each category - each year in this example - should be separated with whitespace to aid viewer comprehension. Within a category, allow columns to touch but not overlap. (There is a type of overlapping column graph called a bullet chart but it is complex to design and often even more complex to comprehend). Also, avoid column borders as there are plenty of ways to visually distinguish each series. I find color provides the best contrast for columns, so avoid patterns as well.

Tip 62: Orient and order legends the same way data series are oriented

Standard, single data-series column charts do not need a legend since the graph title conveys the metric and unit of measure. In stacked or clustered column charts, orient and order legends the same way data series are oriented. McKinsey's slide #6 (Figure 17-3) illustrates this best practice with the legend labels stacked in the same direction and in the same order as the data series. To show why this matters, I intentionally violated this rule in my clustered column chart (Figure 17-4). The legend in that chart would have been much easier to read if "PAEA scheduled pre-funding requirement" were immediately to the right of, rather than below, "Employer premiums." Space permitting, you can do away with legends in stacked and clustered column charts by directly labeling the components in the rightmost category.

Tip 63: Use line charts or scatter charts for trends exceeding ten values

With larger sets of time-series data, a line chart is preferable when there is a clear trend and a scatter chart works better to highlight variability.

In keeping with one of the recurring themes in this book, use every opportunity to highlight the key message with simplification and clarification. Starting with line graphs, leave off symbols unless they provide information critical to the story. If you have multiple time series, differentiate lines with color variation as a first choice and with line style (e.g. solid versus dashed) as a second choice. Shift to scatter plots, choose symbols that are easy to distinguish such as circles, squares, triangles, plus (+) signs, or Xs. Next, enlarge symbols and remove the fill.

Avoiding certain graph types that are inherently challenging to interpret. The area chart for example, the line chart cousin of the stacked column chart, has the same limitation as its relative – namely that one can perceive volatility in the total and in the component touching the x-axis at the expense of correctly interpreting the other components (see McKinsey's slide #11 - Figure 4-4).

Tip 64: Stick to one set of axes per graph

The standard convention for designing graphs calls for putting the independent variable on the x-axis and the dependent variable on the y-axis. By way of refresher, an independent variable is the input, cause, or stimulus. Time is the prototypical independent variable. A dependent variable is output, effect, or response.

The choice of variables determines the units of measure on the axes: Time - the independent variable - measured in years. Revenue - the dependent variable - measured in billions of dollars. While it should be done only in rare circumstances, it is possible to have this one set of axes support multiple dependent variables; both revenue and cost can appear on the same graph.

It is also possible to add a second axis, most commonly a second y-axis as Accenture did on slide #11 (Figure 17-5). Though a good reason to do this must exist, I have not been able to come up with one.

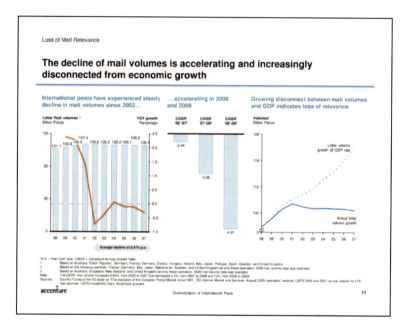

Figure 17-5: Accenture's USPS presentation slide #11

With two y-axes, the viewer needs to spend mental energy figuring out which axis describes which data series. In the leftmost graph in Accenture's slide #11 (Figure 17-5), the point is to convey that international posts have experienced a steady decline in mail volume since 2002. Accenture had two other options available rather than using two y-axes. First, the firm could have just chosen one series; I would have chosen the growth curve since that best supports the point. Second, the firm could have split one chart into two, but that is the inferior design choice here since there is not enough room to tell the remaining two parts of the slide's overall message.

The two-axis problem is a symptom of trying to cram too much information into too little space, thus placing a mental tax on the audience. For this same reason, strive to avoid any type of chart that demands effort to comprehend. My favorite example of a good idea gone badly is the bubble chart in which data is represented not as a point (or other simple symbol) but as a circle whose area represents yet another, usually independent, variable. For instance, imagine a graph with time on the x-axis, revenue growth percentage on the y-axis, and the area of each data point representing total market capitalization. Just because you can do something does not mean you should.

Tip 65: Maintain design consistency across similar graphs in a presentation

Each graph contains a language unto its own consisting of variables and their units of measure, data series formatting, axis orientation, meanings of colors, labeling, etc. As such, each time a viewer encounters a graph, you need to spend a few extra moments explaining how to read that graph so the viewer can understand subsequent graphs more and more quickly. Hence, it is crucial to maintain design consistency across similar graphs throughout a presentation to avoid switching languages on your audience. So when possible, place graphs on different slides rather than cramming multiple graphs with multiple languages on the same slide.

The left and right graphs in Accenture's slide #11 (Figure 17-5) illustrate best- and worst-practice design in action. By way of best practice, the two graphs are visually aligned and consume approximately the same area. Moreover, the x-axis in each graph is identical in every way including the time span of 1998 to 2007, the physical width, the font, and the convention of using only the last two digits of the year. Unfortunately, this is where the best practices end.

The y-axes in both graphs appear to measure the same dependent variable, letter post volumes in billions of pieces. However, there are many differences that may confuse a viewer:

- The axis labels are different; one reads "Letter Post volumes" and the other "Volumes."
- Although the axes are the same height, one ranges from 0 to 120 and the other from 0 to 126.
- Mail volumes are represented by columns in the left graph and by a line in the right graph.
- The word "growth" confuses matters and should be removed from both annotations in the right graph to correctly read "Actual letter volume" and "Letter volume @ GDP rate."

Tip 66: Do not distort graphs

Presenters have a responsibility to design graphs that faithfully reveal the insights in their data. Viewers must never be manipulated into drawing specious conclusions from distorted graphs.

The biggest worst practice in Accenture's slide #11 (Figure 17-5) is the break that occurs in the y-axis. Looking closely, each tick mark appears to signal a difference of seven billion pieces. However, the placement of this break allows the first tick mark to span 105 billion pieces! Breaks are a method of zooming in on the data and have the effect of increasing the perceived volatility in the data. The left graph, whose y-axis follows the best practice of starting at zero and continues without breaks, shows that mail volume between 2002 and 2007 has actually been trending in a very tight range between 106.6 and 105.7 billion pieces, a mere 0.8% difference. By zooming in, the graph on the right makes the change seem much more dramatic.

Breaks are not the only way to use graphs to manipulate the message. Stretching the width of a graph decreases the appearance of growth and volatility and stretching the height of a graph accomplishes the reverse. For axes with positive and negative values, placing the zero crossing anywhere other than the mid-point causes distortions, too (see the YOY growth axis in the left graph of slide #11 – Figure 17-5).

Most numerical transformations are difficult to comprehend by people other than experts. The best example is the logarithmic transformation used for semi-log and log-log graphs, which decreases perceived growth and volatility.

Other transformations live in more of a grey area. Any businessperson should be able to quickly understand a graph of profit over time. Converting the graph to *cumulative* profit over time by adding the profit for a given year to the sum of all prior profits adds complexity and must be explained carefully so that it is not misinterpreted. The same goes for *normalized* profit over time where each value is divided by a baseline value (typically the first one) as well as for profit *growth* over time.

Tip 67: Pie charts are acceptable for composition snapshots of up to five categories

Let's now turn our attention to best practices for designing composition charts. Just like trend charts, composition charts display actual, ranked values or normalized, share values. Since composition charts can only focus on one snapshot at a time, I like to think of composition charts as a way to zoom in on a single column of a stacked column chart.

Pie charts such as the one in McKinsey's slide #8 (Figure 17-6) are an acceptable composition chart option. Many presentation gurus vehemently object to pie charts, but I find them useful in certain circumstances as detailed below.

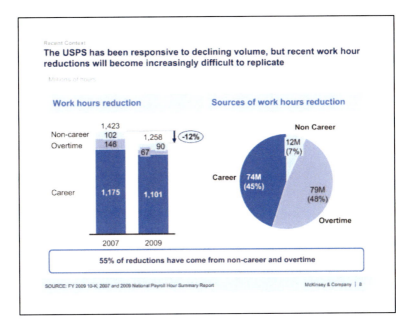

Figure 17-6: McKinsey's USPS presentation slide #8

The stacked column chart on the left side of McKinsey's slide #11 (Figure 17-6) does a nice job of showing the -12% reduction in work hours. However, the nature of the chart makes it very difficult to answer the naturally triggered next story question, "How much of the reduction came from each of the three sources?" That, of course, is where the pie chart on the right comes in.

McKinsey's pie chart is easy to read for five reasons:

1. Every slice uses the same color shade as the category in the left graph.

2. Every slice is clearly labeled. (Avoid legends in pie charts because they require too much work to interpret.)

3. There are not many slices. (Pie charts work best for two to five categories.)

4. The slices are placed in clockwise, descending order.

5. Every slice contains the actual number and percent contribution of reduced hours, making interpretation instantaneous.

Tip 68: Consider treemaps as an alternative to pie charts

Presentation gurus hate pie charts partly because they are so often abused; I have to admit that rainbow wheels do not do it for me either. Nonetheless, gurus also revile them even when every design best practice is followed because the human brain cannot detect small differences in the areas of semi-triangular slices.

Treemaps are an elegant alternative to pie charts and mitigate the perception problem by sizing rectangular tiles in proportion to their data values. BCG's slide #5 (Figure 17-7) is a nice, albeit busy, application of a treemap. Though decades old, treemaps are still part of most presentation design software packages. To create one, you may need an add-in, a standalone software tool, or a lot of patience to do it yourself by calculating rectangle sizes.

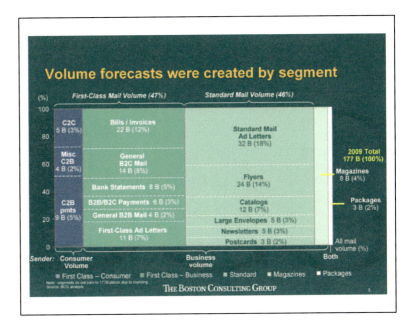

Figure 17-7: BCG's USPS presentation slide #5

Tip 69: Rely on bar charts to depict composition

Bar charts are a foolproof type of graph for depicting composition inclusive of share and rank. While column charts can serve the same function, bar charts allow more space for labels, which is important because text should always be oriented horizontally for better readability.

Accenture relied heavily on bar charts in its USPS presentation, for example the chart on the left side of slide #35 (Figure 17-8).

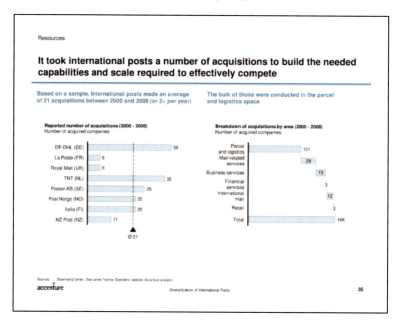

Figure 17-8: Accenture's USPS presentation slide #35

The biggest challenge in designing bar charts is figuring out how to order the categories. The short answer is that categories should be ordered in the way that is most logical to viewers and that supports your message. Of course that short answer does not help you much, so here is a longer one. Determine if sorting in descending value from top to bottom works. This is the best approach if you want to highlight the largest value or one of the values in between the largest and smallest. If you want to highlight the smallest value, sort in ascending value from top to bottom.

Instead of sorting by value, sort labels in descending alphabetical order (as Accenture did) if you expect people to look up particular categories.

If the audience is accustomed to a particular logical ordering of labels, such as by region across a country, sequence in the manner it expects.

Tip 70: Use waterfall charts to show the cumulative effect of changes

Though it looks like a column chart, the chart in McKinsey's slide #12 (Figure 17-9) is actually a waterfall chart used to show the cumulative effect of expected volume and price changes of USPS revenue. To get from $68.1 billion in 2009 to $69.3 billion in 2020, the USPS faces decreases of $11.8 billion from volume decline and $3.8 billion from a mix shift, decreases that are offset by an increase of $16.8 billion from a price increase. Though McKinsey did not do so, I prefer positive changes and negative changes to be shown in different colors for easy interpretation.

Waterfall charts should only be used to explain changes from one level or balance to another - the same way as this McKinsey example. Most presentation gurus would argue, and I agree, that the way Accenture used the waterfall on the right side of slide #35 (Figure 17-8) is incorrect. The Accenture chart should be converted to a standard bar chart with the bar for the total removed and added back as an annotation (n=166).

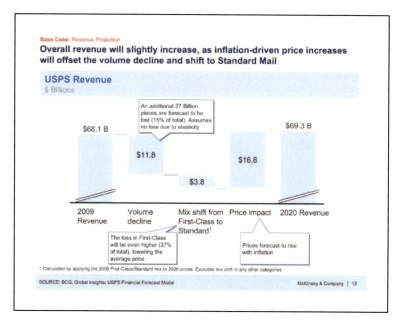

Figure 17-9: McKinsey's USPS presentation slide #12

You will likely need to purchase a third-party plugin to design waterfall charts as most presentation design software does not yet include native capability. I recommend ThinkCell for Windows and Aploris for Mac.

Tip 71: Use distribution charts to show the frequency with which phenomena occur

Distribution graphs showing the frequency with which phenomena occur in defined ranges are a special enough case of composition graphs to deserve to stand on their own. Here, we rely on the distribution graph on the left side of Accenture's slide #17 (Figure 17-10) to uncover best practices including:

- Using ranges equal in size (Accenture broke this rule with 0% and >60% since the other ranges span twenty percentage points. Separating 0% adds value here and in many other instances, but the >60% bin feels sloppy.)
- Limiting the number of ranges to no more than ten
- Avoiding overlap in range labels to prevent ambiguity (Since Accenture used <20%, the next label should read 20% to <40%, and so on.)

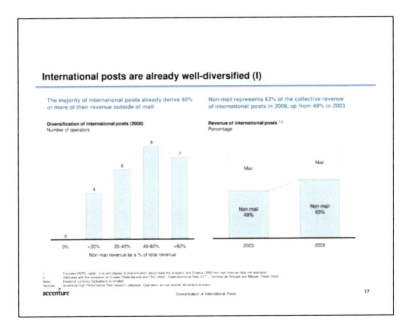

Figure 17-10: Accenture's USPS presentation slide #17

Tip 72: Use correlation charts to illustrate the interrelationship between two variables

BCG's slide #16 (Figure 17-11), showing the interrelationship between mail volume growth and household penetration, is an outstanding example of a correlation chart. The variable that appears to be the independent variable is on the x-axis; the variable that appears to be the dependent variable is on the y-axis. Since an interrelationship is present, the graph includes a trend line that does not extend beyond the range of the actual measurements.

Note that trend charts are a special case of correlation charts revealing the relationship, if any, between a dependent variable and time.

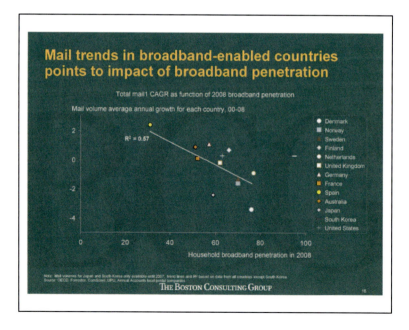

Figure 17-11: BCG's USPS presentation slide #16

The chart title – "Total mail CAGR <u>as function of</u> 2008 broadband penetration" (underline added) - is the honest way to refer to correlation since interrelationship does not imply causation. That is worth repeating – correlation does not imply causation – because any actual cause and effect must be validated through other means. Until that happens, acceptable language includes "as a function of," "points to," or "is (not) related to."

The graph also includes the annotation R-squared equals 0.57, and means that the linear model explains 57% of the variation in the data, a rather high percentage pointing to a strong interrelationship.

* * * * *

The graph types in this chapter comprise the full-set I recommend for designing data-driven presentations. While software allows you to build more exotic charts (bubbles, doughnuts, radars, etc.), I urge caution. The same warning applies to three-dimensional charts of all kinds because it is so easy to accidentally or intentionally distort the data. Stick to the basics and use only charts that are easy to understand and enhance the strategic story.

Chapter 18

Tables

Using tables in persuasive business presentations is rare because, unlike well-designed graphs, tables demand vast amounts of an audience's mental energy to grasp the "so-what". As proof, BCG's and McKinsey's USPS presentations (if you count McKinsey's slide #23 in Figure 5-5 as a table) each contains a solitary table. Only Accenture's presentation contains several tables, further confirming my suspicion that its presentation is really a report intended to be read.

Tip 73: Rely on tables when the audience needs exact values

Viewers can rapidly discern trends and patterns from a well-designed graph. The downside of this benefit is that it is nearly impossible to determine the value of a data point with any real precision, especially sitting ten or more feet away from a screen. If only a few precise values matter, stick with a graph and just add data value annotations. However, when the audience needs to know a larger number of values with precision, tables are your only choice. BCG must have felt exact values for real revenue per delivery point were critical to the audience since it devoted its only table for this purpose in slide #18 (Figure 18-1).

BCG's table illustrates two additional benefits of using tables. The first benefit is the ability to simultaneously show detailed data and summary statistics. In the table, the First-Class Mail and Standard Mail numbers are the detail. There are two forms of summary statistics, the Total Mail values as well as the '09-'20 change percentages. (It is odd that first-class and standard mail do not sum to the total; as a best practice, the detail should foot with the summary.) The second benefit is the ability to mix data with different measures, here "average pieces per delivery point per delivery day" and "real (inflation-adjusted) revenue per delivery point per day (current $)."

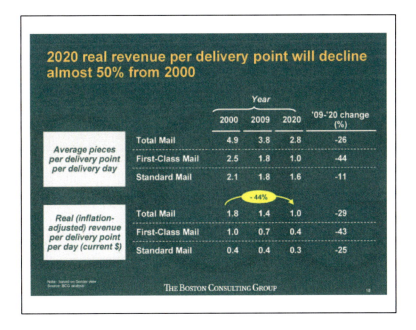

Figure 18-1: BCG's USPS presentation slide #18

Tip 74: Use tables when you need to combine text, data, or images

Tables are also the only option when you need to mix text, data, and images as illustrated in Accenture's slide #37 (Figure 18-2). The formatting of this table allows us to explore several table design best practices as follows:

- Left align words and phrases; right align numbers; center images (including icons, pictures, Harvey balls, checkboxes, etc.) as well as single characters of text
- Numbers should contain commas and equal precision beyond the decimal point.
- Numbers should be rounded to the simplest number of digits while preserving required accuracy.
- Data symbols such as percent signs and dollar signs are optional, provided the rows and columns are unambiguously labeled. For extra clarity, add at least the symbol to the topmost (or leftmost) value in the column (or row).
- Avoid or minimize the use of gridlines. In slide #37, Accenture used alignment to eliminate vertical gridlines and used ultra-thin, light colored horizontal gridlines.

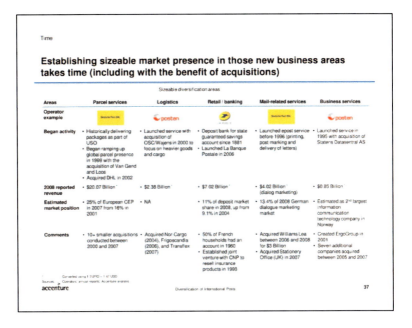

Figure 18-2: Accenture's USPS presentation slide #37

Tip 75: Prioritize the order of table information from top-to-bottom and left-to-right (in Western cultures)

Table information should be ordered the way audience members' eyes scan the slide, top-to-bottom and left-to-right. Accenture closely adhered to this best practice in slide #37 (Figure 18-2). The slide title communicates the core message of the slide – "Establishing sizeable market presence … takes time…" From a storytelling point-of-view, the table must prove the message. Hence, from top-to-bottom, the first and second rows immediately address when specific international posts began to diversify. The remaining rows provide extra detail with "Comments" relegated to the bottom where they belong. From left to right, the four "Sizable diversification areas" get preferential treatment in both location and shading. Though Accenture did not need to do this, switching the text in the "Business services" column would further deemphasize this last area.

Finally, note that eyes naturally gravitate to objects in close proximity. To use this physiological principle to your advantage, space rows very closely together if you want people to read top-to-bottom first, and space columns very closely together if you want people to read left-to-right first.

Chapter 19

Images and Diagrams

Neither images nor diagrams feature prominently in persuasive business presentations, but for different reasons. Images, particularly vivid emotional images prominent in keynotes, are considered too lightweight. Diagrams are perceived as too abstract, too complex, or not data-driven.

For all these reasons, images and diagrams are nearly absent from the three USPS presentations. Nevertheless, the rise of the graphically elegant speaking at venues like the TED Conference is likely to infiltrate strategic storytelling at work, so now is the perfect time to assimilate best practices for designing images and diagrams.

Tip 76: Ensure that images add constructively to your story

Images, more than text or tables or graphs, are the first elements on a slide your audience will notice, so it is your duty to ensure all images add constructively to the story you are telling. If not, leave them off.

Many years ago, office supply stores stocked shelves filled with CD-ROMs of clip art images. These types of images became so popular that thousands of them ultimately came bundled with presentation design software. Today, most people over the age of 10 would not dream of including a clip art image, and certainly not in a persuasive business presentation.

And yet, the more things change, the more they stay the same. The modern version of randomly placing clip art on a slide is randomly copying and pasting images from the Internet that literally or metaphorically represent a concept. As much as I appreciate McKinsey's storytelling and expert graph design, slide #13 (Figure 19-1) exemplifies the merely decorative use of images.

Figure 19-1: McKinsey's USPS presentation slide #13

Tip 77: Put text on image slides rather than images on text slides

The lasting legacy of clip art is that presentation designers got used to putting images on text slides rather than text on image slides. Since none of the three USPS presentations do this, I will illustrate by redesigning the "Delivery Network" part of McKinsey's slide #13 (Figure 19-1). Despite the fact that my resume has the word "marketing" on it, I was trained in semiconductor physics. Consequently, my drawing ability starts and ends with equations and stick figures. So, if I can do this, anyone can. (Giving credit where credit is due, I learned many of these techniques from the talented presentation guru Nolan Haims).

Tip 78: Obtain royalty-free images licensed for commercial use

To start, I need a royalty-free image. Since my photography skills are as poor as my drawing skills, my go-to sources are paid stock photo repositories such as 123RF and iStockPhoto, both of which have great search capabilities and reasonable prices. As a free alternative, most search engines (including Google and Bing) allow you to filter for images that are free to use commercially.

To ensure images are crisp on the screen, try to obtain PNG files rather than JPEGs. For novices, stock photo size choices can seem bewildering. You need the image resolution to match at least the screen on which you are presenting; purchasing a higher resolution image is a waste of money. Since technology is changing faster than I can write, find out the resolution of the screen on which you intend to present. As I write this, projectors in corporate conference rooms are going the way of the dinosaur and being replaced by 720p flat panel displays with a resolution of 1280 pixels x 720 pixels.

It is worth taking a moment to think about what sort of image to use. I already know to avoid cheesy, posed stock photos such as a group of beautiful, ethnically diverse, impeccably dressed businesspeople jumping in the air while smiling and holding hands. Recall, McKinsey's message on slide #13 is that the USPS is struggling to pay the fixed cost of delivering to almost every address in America. The right image should evoke the tone of hard times and of delivering mail unprofitably to remote locales. Figure 19-2, which I licensed from 123RF for $10, captures the sentiment perfectly.

Figure 19-2: Photo of vintage mailboxes in a rural setting licensed from 123RF

Tip 79: Resize images to fill the entire slide

As a best practice, images should fill the entire slide. Unfortunately, the image I licensed has an aspect ratio of 3:2 and most presentation software has an aspect ratio of 4:3. This means the slide will have horizontal bars in the slide's background color at the top and the bottom of the image when the photo extends from the left edge to the right edge.

To get rid of the horizontal bars, I first make the image oversized so that it extends from the top of the slide to the bottom. Since I am very careful to maintain the aspect ratio so as to not distort the image, the photo is now too wide. To fix the overhang, I crop the image on the more visually dense left-hand side to preserve neutral parts of the photo for placing text. The result is shown in Figure 19-3.

Figure 19-3: Mailbox image resized and cropped to fill a slide with a 4:3 aspect ratio

The remaining issue with Figure 19-3 is that there does not seem to be enough neutral space in the sky at the top or the road at the right to pace text. A clever and not overly complex fix is to stretch an unimportant part of the image. If you have sophisticated image manipulation software, which I do not, this is probably straightforward. Here is how I stretched the road natively in PowerPoint:

- Copy the original image
- Paste the copied image directly on top of the original image
- Crop left side of the pasted image to just past the black, rightmost mailbox

- Crop the right side of the original image to the same point, just past the black, rightmost mailbox
- Stretch the pasted image by dragging its left edge even more to the left
- Move the original image to the left so that its right edge aligns with the left edge of the pasted image
- Crop the left side of the original image so that it aligns with the left slide of the slide

The result of all this copying, pasting, cropping, and dragging is shown in Figure 19-4. This is a bit of a distortion, but a small price to pay.

Figure 19-4: Mailbox image with stretched road

Tip 80: Place high contrast text on images

White text usually provides the highest amount of contrast when placed on an image. However, text of virtually any color will fail to stand out on the image in Figure 19-4 since the photo is neither bright nor dark and contains a huge variety of color even in the more neutral areas.

In the final version of the "Delivery network" slide (Figure 19-5), I used two techniques to help text stand out on the image. The slide title uses the easier of the two techniques, a textbox with a semitransparent background.

To allow the delivery network text pop, I darkened the right side of the image using another clever but not overly complex technique. Although artistically imperfect, it is more than adequate for standard business presentations. The trick is as follows:

- Create a borderless, black rectangle that covers the entire right half of the slide
- Change the fill from solid to a linear gradient with each end set to black (at this stage, you will still have a black rectangle)
- Set the angle of the gradient to zero degrees
- Set the left side of the gradient to 100% transparent
- Set the right side of the gradient to 40% transparent

The size and location of the rectangle, as well as the precise setting, will of course change depending on the image and where you wish to locate text.

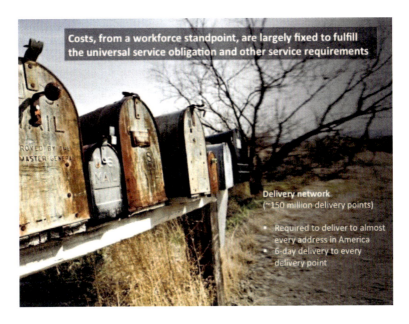

Figure 19-5: Final version "Delivery network" slide

Tip 81: Stick to a single metaphorical system across all images in a presentation

I see many presentations where the designer clearly searched for a succession of phrases and included a sequence of rich, but disconnected metaphorical images; disembodied hands shaking to symbolize trust, a blue sky to symbolize infinite opportunity, and so on. This is the visual equivalent of mixing metaphors and is a big "no-no."

Instead, adhere to a single metaphorical system across all images in a presentation. Given my choice for the "Delivery network" slide, I should use only images with a nostalgic, rural, late-Fall feel in a muted palette. Note, if everything is perfect *except* for the color, there is a good chance the recolor feature included in all presentation design software packages will do a good enough job.

Tip 82: Use diagrams to represent processes, relationships, and geospatial information

Despite the existence of countless standard and custom diagrams, none of the three management-consulting firms used even a single one in their USPS presentations. However rare, there are several diagrams that are extremely useful for conveying certain messages, including:

- Chevron lists: To illustrate sequential processes of flows
- Organizational charts: To illustrate any hierarchical relationship, not only those among people
- Venn diagrams: To illustrate overlapping interrelationships between same sets of items
- Network diagrams: To illustrate structural, but non-hierarchical interrelationships between components in a system
- Maps: To illustrate the distribution of data by geospatial location

* * * * *

In this chapter, I intentionally did not share tips on using video since this media is not often used in persuasive business presentations. While I am smart enough not to say this will never happen, I expect it will be a while until video finds its way into the boardroom for three reasons. First, videos, especially longer ones, allow decision-makers to zone out. Second, videos make presentations feel overly produced. Third, when videos fail due to equipment glitches it reflects poorly on the speaker. Use video sparingly, if at all, until attitudes change and technologies improve.

Section 3:
Confident Delivery

Chapter 20

Verbal Delivery

Tip 83 : Engage your audience in intelligent, authentic conversation

When I write about verbal delivery in keynote speaking, I focus heavily on word choice, repetition, humor, vulnerability, volume modulation, pacing, and other methods to ensure a speaker's voice matches the emotional tone of his or her content from moment to moment. However, this degree of emotional variation and precise language would come off as too over-the-top when delivering a persuasive business presentation. In strategic storytelling, you simply need to allow your knowledge and your authentic, confident belief in your ideas to flow into your conversation.

Here, I stress the word *conversation* even though I have loosely used *presentation* and *storytelling* throughout this book (and will continue to use those three words interchangeably). Business presentations designed to drive a decision should never be memorized nor read off slides or a script. To gain agreement, get the people in the room -particularly the decision-maker(s) – talking early and often. Seek input frequently by asking open-ended questions. Actively read body language as you would in ordinary conversation and ask for confirmation to resolve confusion or objections before they fester.

While you need not know everything, you must actively facilitate to draw knowledge, anecdotes, and stories from the experts in the room. One of the best pieces of advice I ever received from one of my managers was to be comfortable redirecting a difficult question back to the audience (this takes guts but works like a charm.)

Tip 84: Project the verbal authority of a peer

When presenting, speakers get to choose the level of authority they command independent of rank. This means that to secure approval for a business recommendation, behave as a respectful peer. More junior people can raise their authority by: using pauses to eliminate filler words, feeling free to ask questions, slowing verbal pacing, and increasing vocal projection. More senior people must be mindful not to interrupt others, deliver monologues, or speak in a tone that leaves no room for disagreement. Finally, one particularly important but often forgotten practice by all levels of people is to verbally acknowledging others within the organization that helped with specific parts of the analysis.

Tip 85: Take every opportunity to hold the audience's attention when presenting over the phone

Any discussion on confident verbal delivery during business presentations would be incomplete without best practices for holding the audience's attention during a conference call. First, stand while speaking and increase your expressiveness by imagining you are talking to the most senior decision-maker on the line. Second, keep people on their toes (and out of their email and Internet browser) by asking questions of *specific* individuals. Just give those individuals fair warning by saying, "Hey Jane, I have a question for you..." After she unmutes her phone and acknowledges you, ask your question in a way that does not assume she has been paying attention. Using this technique intermittently during a call will ensure everyone stays engaged. Finally, use slides. In fact, use more slides than you would in a face-to-face presentation as slide changes draw attention.

Chapter 21

Non-Verbal Delivery

Tip 86: Manage your fear

Even after working on my public speaking for nearly two decades, I have to admit that managing speaking anxiety is easier said than done. I still feel my heart beating quickly and begin breathing more rapidly before an important business presentation or keynote speech. On my journey, I have found the following best practices liberating.

First, accept that speaking anxiety is perfectly natural and normal. Faster breathing and rapid heart rate pump oxygenated blood to your brain, helping you perform at a higher level. The extra buzz helps you better recall information and answer questions more rapidly. Let go of the expectation that fear ever goes away and redirect that nervous energy into your performance.

Second, accept that you do not need to know everything. All you can do is prepare as well as you can given the time and resources available to you. As mentioned earlier in this chapter, there are many other experts in the room to turn to for support, hopefully including your boss.

Third, release your expectations regarding the long-term consequences of a given presentation. Anxiety, by definition, is rooted in uncertainty. If you start thinking about the impact any single presentation will have on your likelihood of receiving a raise or a promotion, then you are fueling your fear. Focus on getting to the best answer to solve the immediate problem or capture the immediate opportunity, even if the answer is not your exact recommendation.

Fourth, rehearse within reason. Since business presentations are guided conversations, rehearse to internalize the logic and off-slide anecdotes. Additionally, I role-play or ask a colleague to role-play the other individuals I expect to be in the meeting so that I can formulate answers to questions and objections. After I role-play, I pre-syndicate the presentation with as many of the key decision makers and influencers as I can. This is also a golden opportunity to confirm the decision-makers' expectations for the meeting. I know from experience that nothing lowers stress as well as going into a meeting with the deck already stacked heavily in your favor.

Fifth, arrive early to remove the uncertainty of tools and technology. Test your slides in presentation mode to make sure everything displays as desired; this is extra-critical if your presentation includes audio or video. If your meeting requires flip charts, make sure the pens are working. Last, if you will be standing rather than sitting, find a base position outside the projector's- and the audience's line-of-sight to the screen.

Tip 87: Project the non-verbal authority of a peer

The previous chapter outlined behaviors that project the verbal authority of a peer, but to carry them off, those behaviors must also be complemented with non-verbal best practices as well.

More junior speakers have a number of options at their disposal to increase their authority, starting with how formally they dress. In addition, more authoritative people give the illusion of occupying more physical space through using larger gestures and by reducing interpersonal distance (for instance, moving toward the people who ask questions).

Where your seat is located and how you sit in it also matter. Imagine the "power in the room" the last time you were in a business meeting. She was probably seated at the head or near the head of a long rectangular table, showing her hands, and maybe even leaning a little back in her chair.

The way people take notes is also a major sign of respect and authority. Having a scribe take notes projects more seniority, especially if you are standing while presenting. If you take notes, be mindful of the tools you use. In most corporate environments, pen-and-paper notebooks signal the most seniority, followed by tablet computers, and lastly notebook computers, which create a physical barrier.

Finally, take pride in your slides. Developing a presentation takes tremendous research, synthesis, and design work. To ensure you never have to rush through, or worse, skip slides, make every slide count and delete nonessential material or put it in the appendix.

Final Words

The ultimate measure of success of a persuasive business presentation is whether or not the decision reached at the end of meeting is the best one for your company and stakeholders. I hope I have made it clear that strategic storytelling is mostly about what you do *before* you actually speak to a group. While traditional intelligence (IQ) plays some role, I believe emotional intelligence (EQ) plays a far greater role. High EQ, which can be developed, is what makes you a more persuasive public speaker.

Unfortunately, social networking and always-on media have conspired to rob business professionals of verbal communication ability, especially young people joining the workplace. The upside of this modern plague is that individuals such as you, who choose to master the skills of strategic storytelling, can gain a *massive* advantage in the workplace.

Being a more persuasive speaker is the fastest way to transform your ideas into positive outcomes. And, positive outcomes lead to the trappings of career success – raises and promotions. The future of your company and your career are in your hands.

Strategic Storytelling Quick Reference Guide

Section 1: Persuasive Content

Tip 1: Define the problem and make sure it is worth solving

Tip 2: Identify constraints

Tip 3: Build out the mutually exclusive and collectively exhaustive set of issues

Tip 4: Convert your issue tree into a hypothesis tree

Tip 5: Prioritize your hypotheses for impact

Tip 6: "Ghost out" your story on paper using the situation-complication-resolution framework

Tip 7: Test your hypotheses and iterate your story

Tip 8: Title your presentation with a "so-what" encapsulating your overall objective

Tip 9: Make your presentation title SMART

Tip 10: Use an agenda slide to provide your audience with a roadmap

Tip 11: Keep agenda slide titles short and sweet so they can be ignored

Tip 12: Limit agendas to no more than five short items

Tip 13: Add creativity to agenda slide design

Tip 14: Start agenda items with action verbs to signal in which mental mode you want your audience

Tip 15: Apply contrast to highlight the start of each agenda section

Tip 16: Start the situation with the current state of the fundamental issue

Tip 17: To "own the flow," each slide should trigger a question answered by the title of the next slide

Tip 18: Expand on the summary node with depth-first tree traversal

Tip 19: Only go as deep as is needed to introduce the problem

Tip 20: Repeat summary node slides when moving across after going deep

Tip 21: Explore issues and/or opportunities in the complication section

Tip 22: Build up to contentious or counter-intuitive insights

Tip 23: Explore the influence of dynamic trends on the factors discussed in the situation

Tip 24: Deliver the collective impact of the complications on the fundamental issue

Tip 25: Explore the mutually exclusive and collectively exhaustive ways to resolve the complication

Tip 26: Place low-impact resolutions in the Appendix to show they have been considered but ruled out

Tip 27: Prioritize recommendations in impact-, sequential-, or emotional order

Tip 28: Handle objections as they arise

Tip 29: Create an epilogue for critical information beyond the main storyline

Tip 30: Use the Approach-Findings-Implications framework for informative presentations

Tip 31: Avoid presenting the random walk you followed in your research process

Tip 32: Protect your intellectual property and limit your legal liability

Tip 33: Do not include an "Executive Summary" at the beginning of your presentation

Tip 34: Annotations at the bottom of a slide should only be used to transition to the next slide

Tip 35: Prove bold claims

Tip 36: Use ellipses in slide titles to support the flow of the story

Tip 37: Give each slide an independent title

Section 2: Data-Driven Design

Tip 38: Use slides only when they accelerate decision-making

Tip 39: The larger the audience, the simpler the slides

Tip 40: The content in the body of the slide must unambiguously prove the slide title

Tip 41: Match the design treatment in the slide body to the message in the title

Tip 42: Design each slide so that it can be covered in three minutes or less

Tip 43: Use animation sparingly (if at all)

Tip 44: Lay out body content from left-to-right and top-to-bottom

Tip 45: Maintain strict design consistency

Tip 46: Maximize contrast between the text and the background

Tip 47: Use solid colors for slide backgrounds

Tip 48: Use large, standard fonts

Tip 49: Keep text short

Tip 50: Apply a consistent format to your slide header

Tip 51: Craft each slide title as a "so-what"

Tip 52: Convert bullet lists into columns

Tip 53: Use real quotes that you obtained directly

Tip 54: Use column charts for trend data with up to ten values

Tip 55: Title graphs with a "what" rather than a "so-what"

Tip 56: Remove all unnecessary elements from graphs

Tip 57: Use chart annotations in the body of a slide to explain critical inflections

Tip 58: Apply high contrast to chart data that directly supports the slide title

Tip 59: Use a more subtle treatment for forecast data

Tip 60: Footnote sources, critical assumptions, and details too granular for the body of the slide

Tip 61: Design stacked column charts to show an overall trend and its components

Tip 62: Orient and order legends the same way data series are oriented

Tip 63: Use line charts or scatter charts for trends exceeding ten values

Tip 64: Stick to one set of axes per graph

Tip 65: Maintain design consistency across similar graphs in a presentation

Tip 66: Do not distort graphs

Tip 67: Pie charts are acceptable for composition snapshots of up to five categories

Tip 68: Consider treemaps as an alternative to pie charts

Tip 69: Rely on bar charts to depict composition

Tip 70: Use waterfall charts to show the cumulative effect of changes

Tip 71: Use distribution charts to show the frequency with which phenomena occur

Tip 72: Use correlation charts to illustrate the interrelationship between two variables

Tip 73: Rely on tables when the audience needs exact values

Tip 74: Use tables when you need to combine text, data, or images

Tip 75: Prioritize the order of table information from top-to-bottom and left-to-right (in Western cultures)

Tip 76: Ensure that images add constructively to your story

Tip 77: Put text on image slides rather than images on text slides

Tip 78: Obtain royalty-free images licensed for commercial use

Tip 79: Resize images to fill the entire slide

Tip 80: Place high contrast text on images

Tip 81: Stick to a single metaphorical system across all images in a presentation

Tip 82: Use diagrams to represent processes, relationships, and geospatial information

SECTION 3: CONFIDENT DELIVERY

Tip 83: Engage your audience in intelligent, authentic conversation

Tip 84: Project the verbal authority of a peer

Tip 85: Take every opportunity to hold the audience's attention when presenting over the phone

Tip 86: Manage your fear

Tip 87: Project the non-verbal authority of a peer

Acknowledgements

I am indebted to the elite group of individuals who have dedicated their professional lives to sharing techniques for delivering persuasive business presentations, including: Barbara Minto, Gene Zelazny, Stephen Few, Nolan Haims, Matthew Abrahams, and Edward Tufte. Similarly, I have been heavily influenced by thought leaders in the field of keynote presentations including Nancy Duarte and Garr Reynolds.

This book would not have been possible without the encouragement of my super-agent, Jackie Meyer, and the skills of my brilliant editor, PJ Dempsey.

Last and most important, thank you Irene – you are the love of my life. I wish I would write as well as you do and I am fortunate you "volunteer" to edit my first drafts.

About the Author

Dave McKinsey worked in a consulting firm for over sixteen years and is now a writer and business communications trainer. Please use the contact form speakingsherpa.com to reach him.

Made in the USA
San Bernardino, CA
29 November 2018